Praise for *Extraordinary Relationships, Second Edition*:

The timing of this second edition of *Extraordinary Relationships*, a classic in the literature written about the Bowen theory, is fortunate, indeed. Interest in the ideas of Murray Bowen appears to be growing globally, and the demand for accurate information grows with it. Dr. Gilbert's work is clear, accessible, and enhanced in this new edition. It will attract a new generation of interested readers and become a valuable further addition to the libraries of old friends of Bowen theory.

—Daniel V. Papero, PhD, LCSW
Author, *Bowen Family Systems Theory*
Co-editor with Robert Noone of *Family Emotional Process*

Dr. Gilbert's book has become a classic read for those interested in Bowen family systems theory. In a clear, understandable style, her explanations about how families and relationships function are useful in everyday life. For those interested in better understanding family life and one's part in it, this is required reading.

—Anne S. McKnight, LCSW, EdD
Director, Bowen Center for the Study of the Family

After forty years of studying and practicing Bowen theory, I am still de-lighted to recommend this careful, clear, concise examination of the family emotional system based on the original observations of Murray Bowen. Like Dr. Gilbert's previous edition this book is a a valuable resource to people interested in the study of family.

—Eileen Gottlieb, M. Ed., LMFT
Florida Family Research Network

EXTRAORDINARY
RELATIONSHIPS

Also by Roberta M. Gilbert

Connecting with Our Children:
Guiding Principles for Parents in a Troubled World

The Eight Concepts of Bowen Theory:
A New Way of Thinking about the Individual and the Group

Extraordinary Leadership:
Thinking Systems, Making a Difference

The Cornerstone Concept:
In Leadership, In Life

EXTRAORDINARY RELATIONSHIPS

A New Way of Thinking About Human Interactions

SECOND EDITION

ROBERTA M. GILBERT, M.D.

Leading Systems Press
www.hsystems.org

Extraordinary Relationships
A New Way of Thinking About Human Interactions, Second Edition
by Roberta M. Gilbert

Printed in the United States of America

ISBN 978-0-692-82379-8

Book design: Elizabeth Utschig

For copyright licensing, foreign language translation rights, or any additional information please contact:

Greg Jacobs, Editor-in-Chief at
Leading Systems Press
703-336-2754
gjacob03@earthlink.net

See also www.hsystems.org

This book is dedicated to David Gilbert
who first had the idea for this book,
and to readers around the world who want a more useful
and inclusive way to think about human relationships.

CONTENTS

APPENDICES

Foreword—Dr. Murray Bowen

Toward Theory

There have been an increasing number of unsolicited communications about the way lives have been changed by Bowen theory. Many have taken the form of "My life has been different since I learned your theory." There were frequent questions, "What was so helpful?" Responses were as personal as the original statement. The wonderment was often discussed in regular theory meetings. Roberta Gilbert, M.D., attended most of the meetings. She did a paper that combined her own personal reasons about the way her professional life changed after learning the theory. It was detailed enough for the *Family Center Report*, but took the form of a personal testimonial rather than an objective report. As such, it was not publishable. If it were possible to rewrite the paper, eliminate most of the personal pronouns, and put the content into the third person, the theoretical content might qualify for publication. A lesser writer might not have been intrigued by such a rewrite. A new report was submitted within days. It is printed here for the readers.

A good theory is usually an impersonal thing, fashioned from universal knowledge and careful observation. It is usually free of special pronouns, unless used to convey meaning, or unless there is specific reason to delineate self from others in the field. When the overuse of personal pronouns is avoided, the content is framed in the third person, the writing is more solidly theoretical. People tend to dilute theory with personal feelings. It involves mental health professionals too. The dilution has been called the erosion of history. The erosion is present even when the theory is clearly expressed. Dr. Gilbert has made a big step in moving from a personal tribute toward an impressionable theory. The basic theory is different from any other in the mental health field. Perhaps the focus on this one small point will help readers separate disguised personal feelings from theoretical facts. It might contribute a little to authors in the future.

Family Center Report
Spring 1989
Printed with Dr. Bowen's permission

(The paper to which Dr. Bowen referred in this foreword tells a story similar to the preface of this book, although the preface is written in the first person.)

Foreword—Dr. Walter Toman

Historically, Murray Bowen's family therapy must be counted among the earliest practical and teachable forms of psychotherapeutic treatment of families in need and distress.

Viewing the family as a whole in which every individual member affects all others, tracing the members' needs for individuality as well as togetherness, their degrees of differentiation of self and emotional maturity, their relationship patterns and modes of communication, and watching both the system and the process of family life while interacting with the family, have been the hallmarks of Georgetown family therapy. Add exploration of family of origin that the family members are doing for homework, including sibling roles, family constellations, family trees, and communication with all family members. Add, moreover, a family therapist who is attentive and helpful without getting sucked into the family system, and who does not act like a bulldozer shattering the family system or trying to rearrange the rubble. Add free expressions for all family members and an obligation to try to listen, and an atmosphere of warm rationality and calm that the family therapist tends to maintain and elicit.

There is no protracted dependence of family members on the therapist, no extensive regression to early levels of differentiation of self and emotional maturity for therapy's sake. On the other hand, there is no exhibition of therapeutic tricks, no show business, no guru power or manipulation of family by decree. But there is all the independence and autonomy that the family and each of its members can muster and stand, and there is all the respect and tact and sensitivity on the part of the therapist that the family needs.

In *Extraordinary Relationships*, Roberta Gilbert has captured Murray Bowen's theoretical and practical assumptions about the family system, its growth, its disturbances and possible therapies splendidly. She writes with competence, great didactic skill, and from a large fund of clinical and psychotherapeutic experiences. All of her messages are loud and articulate, her practical examples vivid and instructive. This also holds for her concise account of my comprehensive research in family constellation and sibling position and its role in Bowen theory and family therapy.

Summarizing, Dr. Gilbert has written a perfect and unpretentious primer of family relationships. The book is a relief to read, particularly when compared with some of the books on the subject that seem to hide and disguise or confound rather than reveal underlying assumptions, facts, and result, or merely to brag about the fantastic things their authors are doing. Students and even patients of psychotherapy and family therapy will treasure this new book.

Dr. Walter Toman
Professor Emeritus
Erlangen-Nürnberg University
Germany
September, 1991

Preface to the First Edition

When I was first exposed to the ideas of Murray Bowen I wondered if the world of human behavior really needed another theory. Most therapists had all they could manage in attempting to master existing theories, to say nothing of staying current with the seemingly endless variations and updated versions.

I had spent many years in practice using the prevailing psychiatric theories and had concluded that my work was useful to most of the people I served. Yet I believed there was some room for improvement. Perhaps I had an imperfect understanding of the theoretical framework out of which I was operating, or a faulty technique, or perhaps the problem was the theoretical framework itself. I wasn't sure just what the problem was.

The careful and painful exploration of my patients' feelings led to no resolution—only to more and more bared feelings that required extended therapy. Psychotherapy, it seemed to me, was without a goal except that of continued introspection. Dependence on the therapist seemed to intensify rather than diminish as people looked for guidance through the "feelings jungle." And I had few resources with which to approach specific relationship problems such as marriage, child rearing, addictions, or physical illness. These were the very issues most frequently presented to me.

On another level, I looked at the problems of society itself. Crime, divorce, and addiction statistics were climbing. The very existence of the institutions of marriage and family seemed threatened. But theories concerning human behavior did not address those concerns. Whenever I tried to apply existing psychiatric ideas to the social arena, I reached dead ends. Indeed, some of the societal problems, it seemed to me, were exacerbated by concepts prevalent in the human behavior field. Perhaps I could learn a different approach from the small group that was thinking so differently in Georgetown.

Almost as soon as I started studying Bowen theory, I began to apply it in my practice and in my own life. In the beginning I was full of questions and confusion, but I could perceive that I was being exposed to a way of thinking far superior to anything I had previously studied. Gradually, over several years' time, during which I frequently traveled between Washington and Kansas City, the new concepts worked a kind of magic in my life and in my clinical work. As I improved my ability to "think systems," I saw new options for managing myself emotionally. Members of my family sometimes made comments that let me know I was on the right track. Moreover, my patients began to show results that were in an entirely different league from anything I had seen before.

Still, the process of learning a new way of thinking, one that departs from habituated beliefs, is arduous. Once, during one of my many flights to Washington, I visited a friend, a professor of psychiatry at nearby Johns Hopkins University School of Medicine. He expressed amazement that someone at my stage of life and career would go to so much trouble to learn a new theory. For my part, I found it amazing that the profession of psychiatry was not beating a path to Dr. Bowen's door.

Psychiatry, so far, has yet to embrace Bowen family systems theory. This is understandable. For one thing, psychiatry as a profession is inherently conservative. All life prefers homeostasis to change. Furthermore, the new way of thinking is more complex than the old. Indeed, the shift in thinking from existing psychiatric ideas to Bowen theory is similar to the adjustment asked of a child when told, looking out at a flat horizon, that the earth is round.

Just what is the role of theory in science?

Developing a new theory, a profound and radical act, involves reexamining old assumptions and conclusions. It is, in short, taking the first step into scientific inquiry.

A theory is a building block in the development of scientific knowledge. It begins with observation. Observations that do not fit existing theory lead to the development of new theory. If enough factual data are accumulated to support it, a theory is gradually incorporated into science as fact. The idea of the earth being round was once a theory. But gradually, as astronomical and then navigational data were gathered, the theory of the round earth became recognized as scientific fact. The role of bacteria in disease processes was at first a theory. When the microscope was first invented, bacteria were observable, and theory became scientific fact. In biology, the theory of the evolution of species—as first proposed by Darwin—has gained observational support from so many investigators that, although some people see conflicts with their basic assumptions, the theory is very close to being recognized universally as scientific fact.

Bowen's ideas are still at the theory stage of scientific development. Based upon his years of observing human behavior as a psychiatrist, Bowen saw that studying the individual alone and even studying important relationships would never explain all the facts. He postulated a no less radical departure from existing theory than that the family system, not the individual, comprises the emotional unit. Therefore, understanding the family system of an individual as completely and broadly as possible would be the most effective way to understand the individual in relationships.

The tremendous success of current books and presentations about relationships and the family is heartening and may indicate that at least a certain segment of the population is ready to explore the world of the family emotional relationship system. These books and presentations have made use of Bowen theory along with other theories and systems of thought. They have been immensely useful to very large numbers of people, standing in the important place of opening a door on new possibilities.

Some of the essential concepts of Bowen theory, however, have been treated cursorily if at all in some of these presentations and books. Especially conspicuous by its absence is the concept of differentiation of self, the cornerstone of the theory. Systems thinking, of almost equal importance, is also usually left out of most presentations. Many people interested in the ideas of Bowen have asked me for more information about the theory. Specifically, they want to grapple with theory at a more substantive level. They have convinced me that this book would indeed have a place.

The vignettes in this book are not about actual people. Rather, they are composites made up from experiences gained by sitting alongside many real people, observing as they wrestle with living in emotional systems.

Another point is of interest to some. While first names have become commonplace in the therapy world, they are not at Georgetown. Certainly they are never used in presentations. If therapists are addressed by their last names, then it is an invasion of the other's boundary to slide into the informal first name form of address.

I have told my story here in the first person. Many asked that I write the entire book this way. However, in the interest of objectivity, now I would like to get out of the first person. Writing in a relationship style makes contact with people at a certain level. My goal is to define my thinking in the most objective way possible. Bowen theory may become clear without the encumbrances to thinking that a relationship poses. There are already several books in print written from that level. They are useful to an enormous number of people. I have found it even more useful to myself and others to aim for a different level, a level that I believe is more conducive to thinking.

Because Bowen family systems theory is a more encompassing way of viewing the human than we have had until now and, considering the depth of breadth of the human problem at this time in history, I believe it is imperative to communicate what is now happening at Georgetown. For me, and for many people I have seen in consultation, beginning to learn to think from a family and natural systems perspective has been more than worth the effort it took and continually takes. Other theories have had far-reaching impact on the world. It is impossible at this time to predict ways in which Bowen's thinking will impact the future. It is conceivable that the effects will be profound. Much remains to be done. As I see it, we must get on with that work.

This book, then, is a story about what Dr. Murray Bowen, working on making human behavior into a science, learned about human relationships. It does not have all the answers, but neither is it hackneyed or trite. It is based on a new theory. It is not a "how to" book except in the sense that theory acts as a guide for thinking one's way out of enigmas. How-to's have but limited application. Theory has universal application; it can point the way in any situation. If people can develop a better way of thinking and find a better way to manage the self, they can solve relationship, or any other problems as they arise.

Roberta Gilbert, M.D.
1992

Preface to the Second Edition

Considering that the largest percentage of books go out of print in the first year, *Extraordinary Relationships* has done quite well. "ER," as it has come to be called, is still going strong. In fact, it is approaching its 25th anniversary! One might ask, "Why a second edition?"

After working with it all these years—teaching, lecturing, coaching people about relationships, and writing four successive books on Bowen theory—I believe the time has come for a new ER. There are several factors going into this thinking:

- The more anyone works with Bowen theory, the more understanding and facility sharpen. With time there may be a better ability to present the body of knowledge clearly.
- As well, the effort has been heightened by ideas from readers. It is hoped that the purity, elegance, and promise of Bowen family systems theory, as developed by Murray Bowen, is retained.
- The new ER has been edited and rewritten many more times now.
- Structural changes were also needed. For example, theoretical ideas that originally appeared in the first section now seem to combine better with the middle section that takes up ideal relationships.
- There are some modifications. Biofeedback and neurofeedback training have been important to many people and still are. But they, too, are given less space here because they are not always available. Additionally, my experience in practice has been that many of the same effects can be had by simply working on one's way of relating in one's systems.
- Some omissions are remedied. They were always present in Bowen theory, but not in the first ER. One clarification

would be the expansion of the sibling position concept to include and emphasize "functional position." That is more accurately how I believe the subject of sibling position is understood in Bowen family systems theory. Sibling position is only part of the concept as Bowen used it.

- Further, over the years, one of the main demands for a new book has been from academia and other formal and informal groups wishing to make a study of it. Those readers asked for study questions. They are now included at the end of each chapter.

- I also thought that a short encapsulation of each chapter might be of use.

- Because the literature in Bowen theory has greatly expanded in the last 25 years, I have not opted to include a reading list, for fear of unintended exclusions.

The new edition may be slow reading for some in places, though I hope that is less the case than in the old edition. But all who have pursued Bowen family systems theory have learned that "a new way of thinking" can be difficult. If people will consider that fact and make the effort, I believe they will be rewarded, just as so many have been, over time. The promise of Bowen theory, since the beginning, is that of increasingly better family functioning and relationships. With a solid effort and the passage of time, people find that their families, instead of a group to be allergic to, hide from, or run from, become more and more interesting, engaging, and useful to them and to each other. Families become resources for their members instead of a constant challenge. Such an effort also promotes better individual functioning in all areas:

- Relationships improve as people learn to manage their own reactivity and tendency to fuse into relationships.

- Physical health improves as people learn about becoming more of a self.

- People often report more general success in life as they carry with them less and less anxiety over time.

Leaders who engage Bowen theory for themselves also find a higher level of functioning and better relationships within their own families and their work groups.

If this promise sounds too good to be true, it isn't. It comes after many years of observation while many other people, and I myself, do our best to live out Bowen theory. Be assured though, that these wonderful benefits don't come without hard work over a considerable chunk of time. As is the case in most endeavors, what one invests is directly proportional to what one gains.

The new book is organized in three parts:

- Part I, *Relationships We Live In*, (Chapters 1-8) considers the togetherness force that binds people in important relation- ships, especially in families.
- Part II, *Extraordinary Relationships*, (Chapters 9-13) takes up the individuality force: differentiation of self, and what an ideal relationship might look like; that is, one where both partners were perfectly individuated.
- Part III, *Toward Better Relationships*, (Chapters 14-18) goes into some ways of thinking about taking action on self that systems thinkers use in relationships.

At this time, I am surer than ever that we as humans must begin to give relationship science highest priority. We must also get the knowledge of this science into our culture's way of thinking. If we don't, many of our best intellects indicate that the omission may destroy us.

Extraordinary Relationships, Second Edition is part of a ongoing effort to make available to more people a new and better way of thinking about human relationships.

Roberta Gilbert, M.D.
2017

Acknowledgements for the First Edition

A book is the product of many heads and many relationships.

The head of Murray Bowen speaks for itself throughout these pages. He would not have appreciated embellishment.

The idea for this book sprang from the head of David Gilbert, my brother, in 1986, when he asked me to summarize a paper I had just read at the Georgetown Family Center Symposium. He envisioned a book and was so convinced of the value and need for such a work that he gave me no peace until he could see that I was deep into the project. He, a writer, edited, encouraged, advised, and otherwise moved things along. I appreciate his being there, not only in this project but in life.

John Byrd, friend and agent, invested a great deal of himself into this book. He carefully edited, enthusiastically shepherded, and patiently taught throughout long crucial phases. His emotional staying power throughout months of rejections from publishers, and frustrations with my own limitations, has made the difference between the possibility and the reality of a book. Some friends become like family.

Daniel Papero generously and energetically invested many hours and much thinking in this manuscript, right up to the last minute. His great facility with theory as well as with the English language made an invaluable contribution. I am grateful.

Patricia Richter's writing and editing skills made a very positive impact on the manuscript and also on the mind of the author.

Donna Hoel, David Wexler, George Cleveland, Jon Ebersole, and the others at Chronimed Publishing have been enthusiastic, responsible, and flexible through all the difficult phases of bringing a good idea into reality.

Mary Bourne lent useful and practical support in the contracting process.

Virginia Earnest, who designed graphics, was competent, resourceful, and a joy to work with.

Readers invaluable comments have saved the book to such a degree as was possible from overadvising, preaching, name-calling, contradicting, help-giving, exaggerating, and theory-eroding. Their advocacy in many cases added momentum. They are Walter Toman, Michael Kerr, Roberta Holt, Kathleen Kerr, Andrea Schara, Priscilla Friesen, Carroll Hoskins Michaels, Donald Schoulberg, Lina Watson, Jennifer Ashby, Louann Stahl, Marcia Macdonald, John Harper, Bradd Barr, Richard Jafolla, Mary Alice Jafolla, Anne McKnight, Lee Kelley, Susan Willocks, Lisa Egle, Georgia Jacobs, Victoria Harrison, Frank Giove, Robert Gillanders, Janet Kuhn, LeRoy Bowen, Joanne Bowen, Kathleen Bowen Noer, Morley Segal, Patricia Hyland, and my son, Gregory Jacobs.

Acknowledgements for the Second Edition

Elizabeth Utschig merits great appreciation for her skill and patience in readying the manuscript for the second edition as well as for designing the new cover.

Joseph Douglass was a most patient and painstaking editor in the rewriting process. He is sorely missed.

Patti Halbersma shepherded details of the publishing process and is ever faithful in distribution of books.

Paulis Waber improved the quality of the book by carefully and thoroughly proofreading the manuscript.

PART I

RELATIONSHIPS WE LIVE IN

Clinical observations of the entire family together provide a whole new spectrum of clinical patterns never really seen before. . . . Some of the most useful concepts from the early research have remained or have been further developed into the most useful concepts in the field today.[1]

The relationships between family members constitute a system in the sense that a reaction in one family member is followed by a predictable reaction in another, and that reaction is followed by a predictable reaction in another and then another in a chain-reaction pattern.[2]

In broad terms, the togetherness force defines family members as being alike in terms of important beliefs, philosophies, life principles, and feelings. It uses the personal pronoun "we" to define what "we feel or think," or it defines the self of another—"My husband thinks that…"—or it uses the indefinite "it" to represent common values—"It is wrong" or "It is the thing to do." In addition, emotional forces overlap and bind together, assigning positive values to thinking about the other before self, being for the other, sacrificing for the comfort and well-being of others, and showing love and devotion and compassion for others. The togetherness force assumes responsibility for the happiness, comfort, and well-being of others; it feels guilty and asks, "What have I done to cause this?" when the other is unhappy or uncomfortable; and it blames the others for lack of happiness or for failure in self.[3]

[1-3] Quotations are from Bowen, Murray, *Family Therapy in Clinical Practice*, Jason Aronson, New York, 1978, p. 180, p. 206 and p. 218.

RELATIONSHIPS WE LIVE IN

I have developed a family systems theory of emotional functioning. Only a small percentage of people are really able to hear it.[1]

Murray Bowen, 1976

It would be difficult to overstate the importance of human relationships. If love does not make the world go around, then surely relationships do. In the worlds of the personal, the family, the world of work, and the world at large, relationships between and among people are a critical and decisive force.

After air, water, food, and shelter, the quality of relationships most often determines the quality of a person's life. This is true no matter what area of life we consider: emotional, physical, intellectual, social, and, often, economic.

In families, relationship functioning helps people support and cooperate with each other. But groups also carry with them varying degrees of misery. They may blow apart in a veritable "nuclear meltdown."

In the workplace, the outcome of enterprises often depends on the relationships people can establish among themselves. Efficiency, productivity, and creativity are direct indicators of whether people can balance tasks along with their relationships.

In the community of nations, it is human relationships that begin and end cooperation, trade, assistance, and even wars. Further, smooth-running relationships between individuals—in the family, in the workplace, and even in summit meetings—rarely, if ever, happen by accident. Rather, those extraordinary relationships that everyone seeks develop over time when adults relate to each other in principled ways. The problem is that few people have any idea of what the principles might be. Furthermore, well-known and widely taught principles can often add to the difficulty, increasing intensity, labeling people, or framing situations in a negative way.

Often, people settle for relationships that, objectively, are not working very well. The following provide some good examples. Mr. and Mrs. C each had an idea of how relationships should go in terms of housework tasks, finances, and the rearing of their children. Unfortunately, often their ideas did not coincide. So, when one of them would disappoint the other, criticism and blame were the order of the day. The fight was on.

Trying to find a way out of this exhausting and fruitless process, Mrs. C read books about marriage, how to fight, and how to communicate. She found many rules, techniques, and much advice. When she could remember to use them they sometimes diffused the tension for awhile. In the heat of confrontation however, the rules and techniques most often went out the window. Some of the advice actually seemed to intensify the fighting. She became aware, as she tried out each new idea in turn, that something basic was not being addressed—something she had no way to think about.

The D's avoided criticism and blame like the plague. Theirs was a peace-at-any-price partnership. But the cost of not knowing how to address their differences was a distant relationship. If disagreement threatened, the subject was changed or one of the two became quiet, unable to think or speak. They really didn't think of this as a problem. It seemed rather a relief from the turbulent homes each had been a part of as youngsters. They were aware of their discomfort at times. Occasionally they wondered if all marriages were boring and colorless. But their fear of conflict was great enough to stymie any search for a better way.

The O family saw Mrs. O as the problem. Certainly Mr. O's life and career seemed to be on course. If only his wife were in better health. No expense was spared in her medical treatment, but none of it was effective. The more Mr. O tried to help, the worse his wife did. Neither the O's nor Mrs. O's many physicians had a way to think about her ill health as a symptom instead of a disease. A symptom of what? Relationship anxiety.

Mr. and Mrs. T didn't fight. They didn't think of their relationship as boring or colorless. Both had excellent health. But they did not relate directly to each other. They couldn't. Their spare time and attention were riveted to concerns about someone else. Sometimes it was one of their children who was not doing well. Occasionally, one of them became concerned about whether the other was having an affair. They channeled all their relationship anxiety through a third party. Yet, they were not aware of the origin of their anxiety. It was not primarily about the third person. It was about relationship work between the two of them—work that never got done.

Some relationships seem to go very well, with only minimal effort. They seem to flow in a relaxed and enjoyable fashion, with neither partner apparently worrying much about it. They feel most fortunate when they observe the troubles their friends and family experience. They wonder, "How hard is it to just get along?" Such idyllic relationships exist for only a lucky few, no doubt. More often, relationships are delicate and fragile, requiring constant consideration, effort, and a great deal of objectivity.

Relationships do resolve one source of anxiety—that of being alone. But they create another, that of loss of self. Each person feels that too much is being given up or that too much change is required to make the relationship work. And for all the investment that goes into them, the returns for some are slim. In spite of all the creativity, perseverance, and insight they require, relationships often confound and confuse people. They sometimes end in enough disappointment and disillusionment to last a lifetime.

What is missing in the lives of individuals, families, and organizations when they go into a relationship bog-down? Are there guidelines to help plot a course through the perplexing, precarious domain of relationships? Is it possible to attain the ideal of extraordinary relationships now seemingly reserved for so few? What is an extraordinary relationship?

While there is still much to learn, the family systems theory developed by Dr. Murray Bowen offers some new ways to think about improving one's functioning in important relationships. The principles were discovered and developed in work with the human family. But they hold true in other systems as well. The ideas spelled out in the theory form themselves into a kind of "guidebook." It is currently proving itself to hundreds of clinicians working with thousands of people in troubled relationships. These people are able to recognize the freeing aspects of a different and broader way of seeing. It is this expanded perspective that leads them closer to extraordinary relationships.

Let's start our study of relationships by taking a look at the role of emotions "through the lens" of Bowen family systems theory. How do they work for and against relationships?

Emotions in Relationships

> The family is a system in that a change in one part of the system is followed by compensatory changes in other parts of that system.[2]

> There are emotional mechanisms as automatic as a reflex and that occur as predictably as the force that causes the sunflower to keep its face toward the sun. I believe that the laws that govern man's emotional functioning are as orderly as those that govern other natural systems and that the difficulty in understanding the system is governed more by man's reasoning that denies its existence than by the complexity of the system.[3]

Who would want to live without emotions? They inject color, energy, and momentum. They are important to all life, firing the strong, quick reactions so necessary to surviving in a dangerous world. They also make possible procreation and rearing of the young, ensuring continuation of the human species. Survival and nest-building instincts, territoriality, and play, all indispensable parts of the natural order, come from the emotional parts of the brain. Feelings (emotions in awareness) bring not only all these essentials, but also fun, acceptance, and warmth into our lives.

Emotions and Feelings

Emotions are all the automatic reactions, both physiological and mental (another word for instincts), that are generated in the part of the brain humans share, anatomically and functionally, with the rest of the animal kingdom. They are highly complex behavior patterns necessary to the survival of both the individual and the species. For this reason, nature has given them an insistent quality, hard-wiring them into our physiology. They include activities such as warding off or escaping from danger, establishing territory, reproducing, and nurturance of the next generation. The functioning of basic emotional/instinctual behaviors may become impaired as a result of excessive anxiety or illness. And their hard-wiring and intensity make it difficult to voluntarily change them. Emotions can sometimes become so intense they seem to carry with them life and death urgencies.

Some emotionally determined relationship reactions become established early on in one's personal history as patterned behaviors. These patterns may or may not be relevant to the present. For example, a person reared by a father who beat him up after raising his voice may be triggered into life and death feelings whenever he is around someone who raises his voice. Although this reaction is inappropriate to adult life when no harm is threatening, it persists.

Positive emotional patterns are likewise set up. For example, the aroma of pine trees, a smiling face, or the smell of turkey cooking in an oven may all be part of pleasurable patterns preserved in the brain in the same way, associated with a day at camp, a pleasant relationship or a happy holiday.

Somewhat distinct from emotions are "feelings," which are simply emotions of which one is aware. Bowen described the difference this way:

> . . . I regard an emotional system as something deep that is in
> contact with cellular and somatic processes, and a feeling system
> as a bridge that is in contact with parts of the emotional system
> on one side and with the intellectual system on the other.[4]

Feelings and emotions can be triggered by many events and perceptions, whether or not they are relevant to a given situation. They are triggered in relationships on a regular basis.

While they are necessary, desirable, and can be most pleasurable, some old patterned feelings and emotions can lead to difficulties in relationships. Important relationships can trigger strong reactions. These reactions are often hard-wired into us early in life. And many of these emotional patterns established early on may be counterproductive for adult life. In fact, emotional patterns (and the fusions, or loss of self underlying them) are ultimately what can destroy the quality of a relationship.

For the purpose of thinking about systems, it is not necessary to label and qualify all the different shades of feelings that exist in human life. Diagnosis and description of subtle and even obvious differences can lead to a focus on pathology, becoming an end in itself. But diagnosis doesn't change anything. If one thinks instead, objectively and in general terms, of the emotional intensity or "anxiety" that exists in a system, underlying the displays of it, options for managing it become evident. Emotional intensity or anxiety, whatever its expression (whether depression, anger, or even excessive elation) while providing some of the highs of relationships, can also interfere with the ability to be at one's best in relationships.

Anxiety, of course, is a useful and necessary part of the human experience. There is no escaping it. Since anxiety is a powerful teacher and equips us to deal with danger, no one would want to live an anxiety-free life. Anxiety can be acute (short-term), as in a crisis, or it can be chronic, lasting many years or even generations.

Acute anxiety may be triggered by some threat from the general environment, while chronic anxiety is derived from the relationship system—especially that of the generations—and its patterns. But nothing is simple. There are many exceptions to most generalizations. In their simplest forms, acute and chronic simply refer to a length of time. So acute anxiety would arise from short-term stressors, and chronic anxiety from longer term ones, whatever their origins.

Emotions in Systems

In difficult relationships, emotions reverberate from person to person, very much like the excitement caught by a herd, beginning with one anxious individual who perceives danger. In relationships systems, it is as if electrical connections in a group link the individuals of the family, making it an emotionally unified "system," transporting emotions continuously from one to another.

Interestingly, in humans, when one individual excites another, the first is often relieved. In that way anxiety passes like a hot potato, from one to another between individuals, around the group. Emotions are circuited and recircuited, never becoming resolved. This tendency of emotions to travel around the system in a group of individuals who are significant to each other is characteristic of emotional systems. It is part of what identifies a family or other group as an emotional system.

The lower the overall level of emotional maturity in the relationship system, the more this passing of emotions occurs. More emotionally mature individuals are able to be subjected to a larger amount of stress without passing it to others. They can also be around other excited individuals without themselves becoming emotionally excited.

Fusions

Less mature individuals handle themselves differently. Their relationships are susceptible to a great deal of mutual emotional stimulation, partly because there is much "fusion" of selves in their relationships. They carry a lot of unresolved emotional attachment from their original families that goes forward with them into adult relationships. In less emotionally mature systems, relationships serve the emotional purposes of the individuals. The relationship provides emotional stimulation, motivation, and support or other qualities lacking in each partner. One way of dealing with anxiety, for example, is to use a partner for the unloading of anxious feelings. Bowen first observed intense fusions in the research families he studied.

> It was more than a state of two people *responding* and *reacting* to each other in a specific way but more a state of two people living and acting and being for each other. . . . The relationship was more than two people with a problem involving chiefly each other; it appeared to be more a dependent fragment of a larger family group.[5]

Fusions of individuals important to one another make possible the rapid transit of anxiety between them. It is as if they have lost their self-boundaries into a group or relationship self. The passage of anxiety among the selves is evidence of the fusions they are in. To the degree that one is in fusions, one loses self to the system. The fusions exert an emotional pull of the system on one that makes it less possible to be an individual.

Relationship Patterns

These fusions themselves become, in time, a source of anxiety. They are ultimately experienced as uncomfortable, since trying to make a self out of a relationship doesn't work very well. *In order to manage that anxiety, partners begin to posture themselves in recognizable ways. Patterns form.* The four relationship patterns are:

- Conflict,
- Distance and its extreme, cutoff,
- Overfunctioning/underfunctioning reciprocity (originally called "dysfunctional spouse"), and
- Triangling (originally called "focused child")

These patterns are attempts to solve the problem of relationship anxiety. They are not good or bad, they are merely how humans react when anxiety increases. Unfortunately, however, by going into patterns, the basic problem, fusion of selves—emotional immaturity—is not addressed. The same immaturity that led to the attempt to complete a self through affiliation with other selves in the original family is merely played out in ongoing relationship patterns. In that way, emotional immaturity gets pushed into a relationship, becoming a burden on it.

When things are not going well, the human tends to redouble efforts—do more of the same thing—rather than change the quality of the process. In this way, the patterns intensify over time. For example, a couple involved in the distance pattern may intensify its distance to the point of cutoff in divorce.

On the other hand, if *even one of the partners works to get out of the pattern while remaining in contact with the other, the pattern will change,* since a change in one person affects the way the relationship works—for better or for worse.

In the following chapters, we'll take a closer look at each of the relationship patterns.

Thinking It Over

The emotional part of the human, so necessary to survival and reproduction, governs us far more than we realize. When anxiety intensifies, patterns can form and create even more anxiety. They can interfere with the best in thinking, acting, and in relationships.

Real Life Research

1. When anxious, how and where do you experience it?

2. When anxious, what is your default relationship pattern?

3. How do you most often get triggered into emotional intensity?

4. When you were growing up, was your home most often emotionally calm or was it anxious?

5. Can you remember some times growing up when the anxiety level in your home went up? When it went down?

6. Is your life at present mostly calm with more intense periods or is it more often simply more or less anxious?

Endnotes

1. Bowen, Murray, *Family Therapy in Clinical Practice,* Jason Aronson, New York, 1978, p. 387.
2. *Ibid.,* pp. 154–155.
3. *Ibid.,* p.196.
4. *Ibid.,* pp. 158–159.
5. *Ibid.,* p. 10.

CONFLICT

The basic pattern in conflictual marriages is one in which neither gives in to the other or in which neither is capable of an
adaptive role. . . . The relationship cycles through periods of
intense closeness, conflict that provides a period of emotional
distance, and making up, which starts another cycle of intense
closeness.[1]

Murray Bowen, 1976

A conversation with partners of a conflicted relationship often sounds
like this one, with the C family.

Consultant: *What's been happening since we last met?*

Mrs. C: *We have been on vacation, except it wasn't any vacation.*

Consultant: *Care to say more?*

Mrs. C: *It was just constant fighting, bickering and arguing just like we always
have and I am beginning to think, always will.*

Consultant: *What seemed to trigger your difficulties this time?*

Mrs. C: *No matter what I did or said, he would criticize me. I can't seem to do
anything right. I never seem to be able to make him happy no matter what I do
and, frankly, I'm really tired of trying. I think he is just an unhappy person and
is probably going to remain unhappy. Whatever I suggested on the trip—places
to go or where to eat—he would find fault with. He also found a lot wrong with*

me. I don't think we have anything in common. This is the worst marriage I have ever seen and why we stay together is more than I can tell you.

Consultant: *I would like to hear what was going on in your head, Mr. C, while your wife was speaking.*

Mr. C: *She's right. We did have a lot of trouble on our vacation. I don't think I feel quite that hopeless about our situation, but we did argue and fight a lot.*

Consultant: *Any ideas about possible triggers for your difficulties?*

Mr. C: *I just can't handle her ups and downs. Either she's on cloud nine or she's in the depths of anger and depression. I don't know how to handle her moods. I can't get close to her, no matter what I try. It's like she doesn't want to be close. She accuses me of being unhappy. She's the one who seems like an unhappy person to me. I don't even have much desire to be close to her any more. We had one of the worst blow-ups we've ever had about the fifth night of our vacation. That ruined the whole trip for me. The rest of the time it was mostly just petty fighting and bickering, day after day. When she wasn't planning out our whole day down to the last minute, she was threatening to get on a plane and come home without me. I really don't know why I stay around.*

Consultant: *Any idea at all about possible contributions you might be making to getting or keeping this distress going?*

Mr. C: *Doctor, I really don't feel it's my problem. I think I'm just tied up with a disagreeable, unhappy person who has deep-seated problems. I feel she is the one who needs the help. I honestly don't feel I contribute to the fighting that goes on between us. I have good relationships with everyone at the office, with the kids, and with my own family. She is the only one I absolutely cannot get along with. No matter what I buy her or how I change, she complains and bitches, moans and groans.*

Consultant: *It would seem that it might take two to make a conflict, Mr. C.*

Mr. C: *You would think so, but I have changed a great deal. I am really quite easy to live with. Joan refuses to change at all and I'm getting very tired of it.*

Consultant: *Mrs. C, what are you thinking about the conversation your husband and I are having?*

Mrs. C: *It's no different than it ever has been. I think I've made a lot of changes as a result of all the books I have read, but all I ever get from Bill is criticism and put-downs. I can't understand why he can't see what he is doing to me. He really doesn't seem to care.*

These two people are locked into a pattern of emotional ping-pong typical of relationships in conflict. Partners in opposition follow a dramatic course, which inevitably and repeatedly seems to butt them up against each other. They are caught in a war of invective, accusation, and competitive escalation. The pain of their relationship seems to well up and spill out from them, poisoning their environment with distressing regularity. Conflictual partners often deliberately avoid other people, fearing an eruption might embarrass them. Paradoxically, between episodes of conflict they often enjoy a gratifying closeness.

At times of greatest intensity, their relationship may be punctuated by episodes of physical abuse. Theirs is a gut-wrenching, painful life. Other people, observing the chronic nature of their problem, may come to the conclusion that they enjoy this state of affairs. Actually, nothing could be further from the truth. They are intensely aware of their pain. Of all the relationship patterns, people caught in conflict are most apt to seek help to get out of their cycle of hurt.

**Figure 2.1. Conflict diagrammed. Squares represent males;
circles, females.**

Although they tend to blame their partner for their problems, people involved in conflicted relationships may be no strangers to conflict. They may have grown up with it. Sometimes they grew up, not with conflict, but with other patterns that were just as emotionally difficult. It is not necessary to learn conflict or any other pattern. They are built in, automatic parts of the human. They pattern might out in any relationship, given enough anxiety.

Jane Goodall found that conflict and violence broke out among chimpanzees when the leadership was in question. Also, after a large group of the chimps split in two, the two groups later turned on each other in violent aggression. (De Waal wonders if the fact that they had been part of the same group previously actually incited the violence or made it worse.)[2]

Like the other relationship patterns, conflict is an attempt to deal with anxiety, whether it originates from within the relationship or from external triggers. Asked what triggered a fight, one partner sometimes admits "I think I was just trying to pick a fight. I could feel it coming on. It was as though I had to get into it." The greater the anxiety at that time, the more intense the conflict, as is the case with any of the patterns.

People in conflict characteristically show tendencies to:

- Become critical when anxiety increases,
- Become embroiled in blame for perceived problems,
- Project their own problems on other people,
- Focus more on other than on self,
- Fight rather than have fun or do something useful,
- Behave abusively, or
- Use their favorite word—"you."

The most extreme form of relationship conflict is an abusive relationship. Traditionally, they are seen in terms of a "perpetrator" and a "victim." The author noticed a common pattern in several marriages where the wife was hospitalized after abuse. The husband would communicate by way of bluster and anger. The wife would shut down and distance. The more she distanced, the angrier he was. The angrier he became, the more she distanced. So both were contributing to the pattern and either or both, by working on his or her contribution, could change the pattern.

Usually, however, the perpetrator is sent for treatment of various kinds, including expressing his or her anger, which often adds to the problem. Sometimes the victim appears in a help center in such an abject condition that he or she is seen by the helpers as innocent and undeserving of such treatment. The helpers shortly lose any neutrality in their view of the situation. Of course, no one deserves to be physically abused for any reason. But by taking sides, the helping profession as well as the two involved people miss the chance to see how both parties contribute to the problem. The ongoing productive and rewarding way to work (each party working on his or her own contribution) is missed. Thus, resolution takes longer and is less reliable.

How is it possible to change a pattern of conflict? Usually people are told if they will get their feelings out, into words, the conflict will disappear. Unfortunately, people who take this advice find that the more they express their feelings, the more intense the conflict becomes. They also find that the other person really doesn't care to hear that much about how they feel.

Another recommendation to conflicted partners is to learn to fight fairly. Sometimes lists of rules are given for doing this. When a fair fight is described however, it sounds very much like a reasonable conversation and not at all like a conflict. Unfortunately, partners in a conflicted relationship are completely unable to get from where they are to any kind of rational involvement with one another, even with lists of rules. They are so focused on each other and the emotional intensity is so high, that lists of rational rules cannot be brought into play. Awash with anxiety, the cerebral cortex (the rational thinking part of the brain that makes it possible to follow rules) is not functioning reliably.

With only a little reflection, an objective observer of Mr. and Mrs. C would rapidly come to a simple conclusion. *If each partner would discontinue the total absorption with the other and begin to focus on self-management, each would quickly see how they contribute to keeping the conflict going.* Soon the problem would be over. As therapists watch people in conflict, they often think, "If only one of the two could calm down!" Indeed, if one of two conflicted parties could learn to remain calm and thoughtful in the face of the anxiety of the other, there would be no conflict. It actually does take two to make a fight.

But how does one remain calm and thoughtful in the presence of an anxious other who wants to fight? How do they get away from the total other-absorption? How can one get the focus more on managing self? One useful step out, when emotion threatens to take over, is that one can reach for carefully thought-out principles. And of all the useful principles, a first step is to remember that *observing is calming*. Just watching helps us to back off and think more rationally.

When Mr. C was able to step out of the conflict and watch it mentally for a while, his emotional response calmed to the extent that he could see his own part in the problem. At that point he was able to stop making accusations, listen to what his wife was saying, and represent himself in a more reasoned way. *When one can get a little more calm the other will follow in a short time.*

Mr. C began to look into his own family of origin to see what he could learn. This broader, multigenerational view is one aspect of what is called "thinking systems."[3] Many times he had vowed that his marriage would be different from that of his conflicted parents. And yet, here he was, firmly embedded in a relationship posture very similar to that of his parents. The emotional patterns in his family of origin had, over time, become a part of his own personal emotional reflexes, hard-wired in. Sometimes people blame their families for their patterns. But as adults we have choices if we are willing to work on self. Mr. C used his research to see that, although conflict was an emotional pattern he was used to, he actually had other choices for managing himself when the anxiety cranked up. Later on, he would go into his conflicted family of origin and make some substantive relationship changes as he became more the observer and less a participant in those patterns.

Another way Mr. C tried to think systems was by looking at a bigger picture, to adopt a broader outlook than simply his immediate situation. For example, on their next vacation, when small issues threatened to erupt into conflict, Mr. C was able to put them in perspective by mentally removing himself from the anxiety generated by the relationship. He would place himself in the context of being on vacation. Keeping in mind the systems of people around him—their work systems, their families, their community circumstances—he became fascinated by the place he was visiting. His stay with his wife, put into a systems context, turned every happening into an adventure, bringing a movie-like quality to the trip, with the C's as the stars.

Mostly, he began to focus on his own behavior: observing verbal and nonverbal signals that indicated how and when he himself was escalating emotionally. Just getting into the observer position is calming because it requires cerebral—thinking—activity. *Whenever the cerebral cortex is activated, the emotional centers are inhibited.* From a position of watching, he could see what, on his part, would calm and what would intensify the conflict. With effort he began to make better choices in interacting with his wife.

When one person can calm self to some degree in the face of the other's anxiety, keeping good contact, over time the other will join the first at a better level of functioning. That is what it takes to improve the quality of the interaction between the two.

Mr. C would also think of another principle—the range of adaptability that exists among people. This thought reminded him that he had a choice between thinking and feeling. In a spectrum of possible responses, some of his own might be less mature, less thought-out and more emotionally reactive than he would like. But he could formulate what a less reactive response might be. He could see he had been repeating his old immature behavior patterns. When he felt anxious he would usually find someone to blame. Something about being in a fight had previously had the effect of calming him. Also, he usually won the fights. Winning somehow bolstered his self-esteem.

Working toward a higher level of relationship functioning would mean finding new ways of thinking about himself and of calming his anxiety. When his anxiety reached a certain level, he fought, as if by reflex. Doing better in the family system he and Mrs. C had created meant he would have to find a way to stay calm when she was upset and continue listening to and talking with her. Since trying to change another person is an exercise in futility, Mr. C had to learn to stay on track with himself. He had to learn to suspend all criticism, censure and challenge, attempting always only to manage himself better emotionally.

The task of changing a conflicted relationship into a more smoothly functioning one might seem impossible. One or both people sometimes have had years of involvement in, or exposure to, conflicted relationships. Since patterns are highly resistant to change, Bowen experimented with a radical idea. He asked people, instead of simply talking about the problem with a therapist, to take their patterns back into the family system in which they developed in the first place—the family of origin—and change them there. Often, that effort produced more worthwhile results than efforts toward the present relationship. The good results happen not by trying to change the people in the family, but by attending to one's own reactions to family members and finding different ways of relating to them.

The brain is a social brain. So, when we make changes in our important relationships, brain functioning thrives. When that happens, our cell physiology of the body improves as well.

Mr. C worked on changing his own emotional patterns within his family of origin by visiting his family more often. He also called and wrote more often. In the beginning, he automatically reacted when his parents began their conflicts. After gaining some skill at watching that pattern within himself, he was able to observe their intense behaviors without taking part in them. Later, he was able to converse calmly and thoughtfully with them, whether or not they were in conflict. This work took place over several years and demanded much thought and effort. But over time, all of Mr. C's relationships improved as he learned to better manage himself emotionally around his parents. He stopped blaming. His temper, which had always been notable, was less in evidence. His relationship with his wife became calmer and more thoughtful, as well as more fun. His children benefited immediately from a different home environment.

When a fight or argument brews, what can one do about it? What can be done or said that does not contribute to the pattern? For one thing, one can begin to watch the reactivity in self. *Just watching is a calming activity*. And calm, thoughtful, careful watching can often inform significant changes in one's own part of the relationship pattern.

The ultimate goal is to react less intensely and to continue to stay in calm, logical contact with the other person. This is not easy to attain in an intense situation, but simply having the goal in mind can inch people along.

Tiring of conflict, people often retreat into distance. And sometimes both conflict and distance become an alternating, predictable pattern. Distance will abort the conflict externally. Unfortunately it often continues internally because distancing does nothing about the underlying fusion. The over-focus on the other continues. Unfortunately, *distance itself is an emotionally patterned reaction.* We will take a look at it in the next chapter.

Cesar Milan, the "Dog Whisperer," so savvy about the emotional brain from his years of working with out-of-control pet dogs, talks about the "red zone." When a dog just begins to get excited (yellow zone—caution!) it is time to put on the brakes. Once it gets into the "red zone" it is too late. Nothing will work.[4]

It is most useful for us humans to monitor and regulate our own emotional states in a similar manner. If we can learn to think of calming ourselves when we start going into the yellow zone of emotional intensity, where we still have a modicum of control, we can usually learn to avoid the destructive red zone, where thinking, feelings, words, and often, behavior, only escalate to the point of no return.

International conflict is called war. It has often been said that war has never solved any problem. If nations, in the forms of their negotiators, could think in terms of staying calm, rational and in contact with each other, could most wars be averted? Bowen theory would seem to indicate that they might.[5]

Thinking It Over

Conflict in the wild determines winners and losers and ultimately, a hierarchy. In humans, too, competitive conflict can be fierce. Most often, though, it is inappropriate and unnecessary. When one person can stop being triggered by the anxious other, over time, by staying in contact, the other will shortly join the first at a better level of functioning. That focus on one's own functioning is what it takes to improve the interaction between the two.

Real Life Research

1. In your family of origin, how were disagreements handled?

2. Have you adopted those patterns —or reacted to them?

3. How do your children (or nieces and nephews) handle disagreements?

4. How is the blame game going on in society at large?

5. How often do you use that favorite word of conflicted relationships: "you?"

6. How does conflict play out in your workplace?

7. How many conflicts do you see in the world at large at the present time?

Endnotes

1. Bowen, Murray, *Family Therapy in Clinical Practice*, Jason Aronson, New York, 1978, pp. 377-378.

2. de Waal, Frans, *Peacemaking Among Primates*, Harvard University Press, Cambridge and London, 1985, pp. 71, 247.

3. "Thinking systems" simply means a bigger picture, that of the entire relationship system, that takes into account as many of the players and their patterns, in

relevant systems, as may be pertinent. Systems thinking will be elaborated in more detail later.

4.   For more on this topic, see https://www.cesarsway.com/dog-behavior/aggression/understanding-aggression.

5.   Farren, Sean and Robert F. Mulvihill, *Paths to a Settlement in Northern Ireland.* Oxford Press, New York, NY, 2000.

3 DISTANCE

There is a spectrum of ways spouses deal with fusion symptoms. The most universal mechanism is emotional distance from each other. It is present in all marriages to some degree and in a high percentage of marriages to a major degree.[1]

Murray Bowen, 1976

The D's also went on vacation—to the Bahamas to attend a professional meeting. Lying on the beach, her eyes focused on the sparkling waves, Mrs. D was deep in thought. She and her husband had a good life. They had few financial worries. Mr. D had done very well with his firm and in a few years, he would retire. The children had been Mrs. D's primary responsibility. Mr. D had stayed relatively uninvolved, especially in the early years, because his job had required him to travel a great deal. At times, Mrs. D wished her husband had been more a part of the children's growing up. It seemed that the crises always occurred when he was out of town, but she had learned to cope and actually became quite proud of her ability to manage whatever came up. But now the offspring were well launched and, on the whole, doing quite well.

Unlike some of their friends, the D's relationship had survived the kids' teenage years. This thought cheered Mrs. D during times when her anxiety focused on her marriage. Sometimes, though, she found herself wondering what she would do with him under foot after his retirement. What would they talk about? He had been absent so much through the years that she wondered if they really knew each other. Would they tire of each other if they were together more?

Her thoughts were interrupted abruptly as her husband shook cold droplets of water all over her after his ocean dip.

Later, he napped and she walked the beach alone. Again, she thought about their relationship. She could not shake the nagging idea that she was afraid of his retirement, dreading having him around all the time. As she followed this line of thought, she started to feel very guilty.

That evening, they ate lobster, danced to the island music, and chatted with other couples they met. Mrs. D never seemed to find a time to talk about her concerns. They seemed so negative. She feared they would ruin a good time. After all, life was actually pretty good. That night, she lay awake wondering and worrying about why she and her husband never talked about anything really important.

The next day, her thoughts went to all the parts of life they had never shared. During the early years of their marriage, Mr. D was gone a great deal, making a living for the family. She was home alone with the children. They had done pretty well with that arrangement. She had no idea what their financial position was though and, if she ever had to, no knowledge of how to manage the money. Whenever she broached the subject, he would only say, "Don't worry about it." Did he fear his own mortality, or did he just dislike discussing finances with her?

Why was it so hard for them to get beneath superficialities? She tried to think of ways to get through to him to ask her questions and express her concerns. Perhaps he would listen to her if she were more intense, pleading, or assertive. Perhaps, if she showed him more attention, he would make more contact with her.

When they returned home, she tried all those things. None of them worked very well. The more she tried, the less he seemed to engage. The more she pushed for answers, the less he was actually home. He was either playing golf, cards, or traveling for his work. Distance had become a pattern—an unspoken rule by which they lived.

Though it is possible to see distance in all the other relationship postures, this couple's story is common enough to warrant definition and description of distance as a pattern distinct from the others. The meaningless aloofness of these partners stands in sharp contrast to the intense expressive type of involvement seen in the conflicted one. Distance is so common that it may not be seen as a problem. While the partners experience inner pain, sometimes of great magnitude, they more often tend to deny it, seeing the position as normal. They may perceive their relationship as an improvement over that of their parents. They may even see it as giving "space" to the other. And at times, for brief periods, it may be useful.

Distancing may take several forms, so there are several ways to diagram the posture. One partner may distance in response to the other's pursuit. The more partner A pursues, the more B distances, eliciting more pursuit in A, and so on and on.

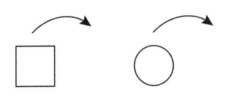

Figure 3.1. The pursuit-distance form of distance.

Or, both may be distancing overtly.

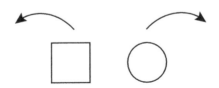

Figure 3.2. Both are distancing.

Another way to diagram distancing, emphasizing the intensity leading to it, is by showing several lines of intensity cut off by the distance.

Figure 3.3. Distance, another form of emotional intensity.

It is important to note the little intensity lines in the diagram. The intensity of the fusion is what leads to the distance.

Although one of the partners usually gets labeled as "the distancer," both (as is the case in any relationship pattern) play their part in it. If the pattern is one of pursuit and flight, the pursuer plays his or her part just as surely as does the fleeing partner. The pursuer may complain long and loud about "the distancer," but the pursuer is making his or her own contribution to keeping the distance pattern in place. The flight may be a reaction to being pursued. If so, the distance pattern can be resolved when the pursuing is stopped or lessened.

Distance in a relationship can give rise to other problems. Often a person whose partner is distancing can become very jealous, convinced there is a triangle or he or she is "unloved." If one partner distances into work, the other may actually become jealous of the work situation, which can come to be seen as the problem.

Besides overwork, distancing partners often take refuge in substance abuse or jobs requiring travel. (This is not to say, however, that all people in careers involving travel are in distant relationships.) The ultimate form of distance is cutoff.

Signs of distancing include:

• Excessive periods of no communication,
• Workaholism,

- Overuse of substances such as alcohol,
- Excessive time spent on hobbies,
- A tendency to be quiet when anxiety rises,
- Talk that includes nothing of personal importance, and
- Lack of knowledge about or little contact with the people in one's immediate or original family.

Divorce is often seen as a resolution to an otherwise insoluble problem—a relationship that doesn't work. Often these partners are involved in a conflict/distance merry-go-round that never ends. Each, blaming the other, comes to believe that the relationship isn't worth working on and the only way to get peace of mind is to go their separate ways. Neither sees how self is contributing to the continuous intensity.

People involved in a distant relationship sometimes see their own distancing as an attempt to help the relationship in some way. Or there may be a manipulative use of distance, in an attempt to draw the other in. Sometimes, distance is an attempt to get far enough away from relationship conflict to gain control of one's own emotions again. Frequently, alternating conflict and distance becomes the pattern. Distancing partners may not trust themselves to relate to each other at all until the intensity abates. They may be guarding against the possibility of conflict they grew up with in their families of origin. Distance, for them, may seem like a relief. Growing up in a conflicted family, one may have learned to distance from the turmoil at an early age. Most often, distance seems to be an automatic attempt to make the relationship tolerable by getting periodic relief from its emotional intensity.

Unfortunately, the attempt to make things better for oneself or the relationship through distancing is rarely successful for long. Outwardly the partners express distance towards each other, but inwardly they maintain an intense focus on one another and the relationship. Distance can provide some temporary emotional calm, but over time, like the other patterns, distance *actually intensifies anxiety.*

As with conflicted relationships, distancing partners may be able to find this posture in many relationships in their families of origin. They may have had (and have) only superficial or meaningless relationships with their siblings. Or their parents may have had a distant relationship pattern that they adopted. Often the pattern can be seen in many generations of a family, as a kind of lifestyle. But all of the patterns are within each of us, innately, ready to spring into action, regardless of our family experiences.

How does one begin to think one's way out of a distant relationship? Stepping back to take a good long look at the relationship over time can be instructive. How did/does the pattern emerge out of anxiety? How effective is it at managing anxiety? How much does distancing contribute to anxiety? When Mrs. D took an objective look, she realized the chronic distance pattern in her marriage had generated more anxiety than it had resolved. She had no idea how it began but she knew that for many years the distant pattern of her marriage did not seem like a problem. It seemed a step up from the conflict of her parents.

In time, however, she wanted to try for more meaningful contact with her husband. When making contact around important issues became a priority for her, she found ways to relate differently. But first, she observed that at a point when anxiety became especially intense for her, Mrs. D did what is often advocated as a way of managing feelings: she told her mate about them with a great deal of feeling. The more her feelings spilled out to him, the more he would distance. As the process of their pattern became clearer, she was better able to see what her part in the distance was. As she began to see how others, especially her husband, reacted to her intense way of presenting herself, she realized there might be other ways to approach him. Her work had just begun. A great deal of practice is required before new patterns become part of the working emotional repertoire.

Gaining objectivity about one's relationship postures certainly involves thinking systems and gaining as much understanding of one's own systems as possible. The effort involves asking many hard questions:

- "How do I distance from my extended family?"
- "How do people in my family distance from each other?"
- "How many distant relationships can I find in my family of origin?"
- "How do I distance from my colleagues at work?"
- "How do I distance from my friends?"
- "How do I get them to distance from me?"

An even better question is: "What is the origin of the anxiety that leads to the distance?"

As those intense reaction patterns are better understood, the need for distance may become less pronounced. As with all the relationship patterns, simply taking a look through the lens of family systems principles can lend objectivity about one's own role in the process. That objectivity can inform positive steps to change.

If distancing is seen as an attempt to deal with the anxiety created by relationship fusion, the question becomes, what efforts would be more appropriate than a pattern that simply intensifies the emotional problem? Mr. and Mrs. D found avoiding meaningful contact with each other was deadly, not only to their relationship, but to the individuality of each. When they began to experiment with being in better contact on a more regular basis, (only briefly, in the beginning) they found they had more freedom to work on their individual life issues than they did when they avoided the relationship by habitual distance.

If a relationship is stuck in feeling intensity, disguised outwardly by superficiality, silence, and avoidance, it is important to get in touch with the emotional intensity that underlies the distance. If one does not, to some degree, differentiate self from the togetherness fusion that generates that intensity, one will usually try another relationship posture in the interest of doing something different. The solution for a relationship posture is not another posture, however, nor is it intense smothering closeness. When Mrs. D understood that, in her marriage, distance was partly a reaction to her own emotional intensity, she could see the importance of managing herself differently. As she dumped less emotional intensity into the relationship, she perceived less distance from her husband. This was calming to her, so a different, more productive kind of relationship interaction developed.

Her changes were not as reliable as she hoped until she took a long look at the family she grew up in and worked to change her reactions there. During her childhood, her parents had a conflictual relationship. When fights would break out, she would cover her head with the bed covers or hide in a closet. In her teenage years, her parents divorced. After that, she and her three younger siblings saw little of their father. She developed a rich fantasy life about creating a different kind of family. "How hard could it be to create a normal family?" As an adult, with avoiding conflict as her only guiding principle, she found herself and her husband simply avoiding each other.

Her work began with an effort to bring meaning, not only into her relationship with her husband, but also with her mother. She had only a superficial relationship with her mother, fearing the kind of conflict she witnessed between her mother and her siblings. Now, without blaming or trying to change anyone but herself, she dared to ask her mother questions about the generations of her family. Some questions were unwelcome, especially those about her mother's parents' relationship, her mother's relationship with her father, and about her father's family. The effort led, of course, straight towards conflict. Mrs. D anticipated it and was prepared. She met her mother's reactions with calm, thoughtful responses. These became easier the more she understood her mother's place in her own emotional system.

In time, she even made contact with her father, whom she had not seen for several years. As she came more into contact with him and his family, the other fifty percent of the intensity in her original family became clearer. As she continued the hard work, over years, of getting into the emotional field of her extended family and becoming more the present and responsible self she wanted to be in it, her reactions in her own nuclear family were less intense. She had more choice in the midst of reactivity. She gained, over time, more ability to think her way through emotionally triggering events, avoiding her tendency to run or hide from issues. She was, in short, *more of a self*.

Simple, calm, person-to-person contact is elusive for many people. Learning how to make meaningful human contact after a lifetime of distancing is no easy task. For those in a distant relationship, it is sometimes useful to try to make a point of having a little more contact with the other person for even a few minutes out of every day. Letting the other person know what is going on inside one's head is balanced by listening to the other, attending to verbal as well as nonverbal clues. Most distanced partners will not tolerate more than short periods of contact in the beginning. However, over time, they often find that their reactivity decreases.

What is meaningful contact? It is hard to define, but people do know when they have or have not made contact.[2] It is something that other animals are good at, judging by various reports from ethologists who talk of apes extending an open hand to one another, of grooming, or of sexual contact.[3] Sometimes it seems that humans have lost the art. The range of possibilities for contact open to human beings is extremely large, ranging from conversations that can last hours to something as brief as a pull on a pigtail. However, the attempt to make even brief contact with the other on a regular basis can put a distant relationship back on track.

Thinking It Over

Staying in contact with important others takes a great deal of effort for some people and in some families. But that effort is richly rewarded by a less anxious, more productive brain and life and often, a better functioning relationship system.

Real Life Research

1. On your family diagram, can you spot distant relationships?

2. How many divorces are there?

3. How many immigrations can you find where those involved did not stay in contact?

4. How do you promote distance in your relationships? How do you see this coming out of your original family experience?

5. Who are you distant from in your family of origin?

6. How about your workplace?

7. What triggers distance for you?

8. What would be instances of distance in international relations?

9. What promotes it?

10. What steps could leaders of nations take to promote less distancing between and among nations?

Endnotes

1. Bowen, Murray, *Family Therapy in Clinical Practice*, Jason Aronson, New York, 1978, p. 377.

2. A point often made by Kathleen Kerr in lectures at the Bowen Center for the Study of the Family.

3. de Waal, Frans, *Chimpanzee Politics*, Johns Hopkins University Press, Baltimore, 1982; and *Peacemaking Among Primates*, Harvard University Press, Cambridge, MA, 1989. Both contain many descriptions of overcoming distance among animals.

CUTOFF

The principal manifestation of the emotional cutoff is denial of the intensity of the unresolved emotional attachment to parents, acting and pretending to be more independent than one is, and emotional distance achieved either through internal mechanisms or physical distance.[1]

Murray Bowen, 1974

Mrs. U had been on antidepressants for years. When her family physician refused to keep her on them any longer without psychiatric consultation, she agreed. The psychiatrist asked about her family relationships and found that Mrs. U was very close to her grown son and his family. In fact, she could be said to be devoting most of her life's energy to that family, helping them any way she could. She baby-sat, cooked, cleaned, and, in general, spent a great deal of time in their home. Her marriage was stable if a little distant. Most of her family of origin was deceased, although she had one sister living in a distant city whom she had not seen in years. She told the story of the hurt long ago when this sister had remarried and left town with no explanation, never contacting the family again.

That hurt had apparently stood in the way of Mrs. U's making contact with her sister for many years. She was definitely not motivated to be in touch with her in the beginning of the consultation. The psychiatrist wondered if the depressive symptoms she was experiencing could possibly be related to the cutoff from her sister and other members of her family. Mrs. U became intrigued by the idea that her symptoms might improve if she made an effort to bridge the cutoff with her sister.

Mrs. U summoned up her courage and sent a friendship card with a brief note to her sister. In a few days she received a long, warm letter. Correspondence continued, followed by phone calls. Finally, they made plans for a reunion. After that, Mrs. U noticed that her antidepressant medication was too strong: the dose had to be lowered repeatedly. Within a few weeks she was off the medication. As her efforts expanded to contact other family members she could locate, her depression continued to recede. Since many physicians had told her that she would probably always need antidepressants, Mrs. U was amazed and delighted when the need for them disappeared.

Cutoff is the extreme of the distance posture. But it is so important and prevalent, so much a part of and a factor in our society, that Bowen gave it the status of a separate concept in the theory. It was originally described to mean cutoff between generations. But it came to mean the disruption of any important relationships. Quite often the cutoff is so old that the people involved have forgotten what originally triggered it.

If there is more than a quantitative difference between distance and cutoff, it may be one of focus. In distance the two are preoccupied with each other, though in diminished contact. With cutoff, the partners may think of each other rarely, if at all.

America has sometimes been called a nation of cutoffs, having been settled largely by immigrants. Not all immigrants cut off from their families, but it is thought, from clinical observations, that a large percentage do. Though that question is still being researched,[2] family therapists are quite sure that cutoff is such a common phenomenon among American families that it is often hard to see.[3] It is often seen as a desirable state of affairs, or as the lesser of the evils.

For whatever reasons, it does seem that, commonly, the American way of growing up is to leave home and never return again, emotionally speaking.[4] When one leaves home, meaningful relationships with one's family of origin are often severed. Visits are limited to those of the "duty" or "ritual" variety around holidays.

Events immediately preceding the cutoff may be erroneously viewed as "the reason" for the cutoff. These "triggers" can include, among many others, disagreements over inheritance at the time of a death in the family, religious differences, or side-taking around and even before a divorce. These precipitating circumstances stand out as "the cause" in the minds of people who are cut off from each other. In fact, however, issues at the time of cutoff are rarely the issue.

Rather, the problem is *unresolved emotional attachment,* or *fusion.* Thus, the real difficulty goes back much beyond the time of the cutoff itself. It is, like the other relationship patterns, an attempt to adapt to the chronic and acute anxiety that those attachments generate.[5] When we look at the family diagrams of people with this pattern, we usually find that there is more than one instance of cutoff in the family. In fact, most often, many generations will have taken part in the same patterned response to intensity. It is only one end point in a long-term generational family emotional process.

Looking at the family process for as many generations as possible carries a great deal more benefit than simply seeing the latest manifestation of it. Over and over, fusions of selves in the nuclear families have led to anxiety that is triggered around some issue. Yet, because the intensity of feelings makes it impossible for anyone to think clearly, individuals respond with emotionally based action—the family's knee jerk reaction pattern—cutoff. The family immaturity thus moves one more time, through one more generation.

"Issues" may provide the setting, but the unresolved family fusions are actually the problem. In a more mature group, or under less intense conditions, these issues get handled in a way short of cutoff. Unfortunately, what the individuals who are cutting off don't understand is that there is a very dear price to be paid for emotional cutoff.

Cutoff can ameliorate emotional intensities or symptoms temporarily but, over time, it actually increases them. That is why, with the exception of a brief period of calm (or even euphoria) immediately following the cutoff, people involved in cut off relationships begin to experience an intensification of anxiety (in whatever form it may take). They find themselves with symptoms such as being socially adrift, depression, suffering from addictions, or getting embroiled in legal entanglements. Sometimes there is merely a general failure to succeed. *The brief period of euphoria after the cutoff throws people off track.* It is the deceptive part of the pattern that prevents an understanding of the link between the cutoff and the later emotional symptoms. Because the actual cutoff is removed in time from the onset of symptoms, the link between the two is not usually perceived.

Cutoff is linked with poor relationships in other parts of life. That means that relationships in the workplace, friendships, and even love relationships will not be as smooth for people who are cut off from their families of origin as they are for people who are in better contact. Because the emotional systems of cutoff people tend to be smaller, the relationships they do have are more intense. Anxiety in the system has fewer places to go. A pattern of cutoff is like a cancer, spreading into all areas of life.

Cutoff can be diagrammed as follows:

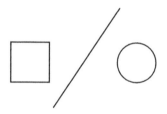

Figure 4.1. Cutoff.

Consider a generic opera plot. The tenor and the soprano meet. They are instantly attracted. They fall in love. They are full of fervent, passionate feelings that are lyricized and dramatized on the stage. But alas, almost as suddenly as their passion develops, another mood appears. Now, the fervent, passionate love turns into fierce, fiery rancor. Invectives are hurled. The two separate and go their singular ways into the world. As they wander the earth for years, they never cease to think of one another. They dream and fantasize about each other. "If only I could be back with him (her), my life would be wonderful!"

One day, completely by chance, they meet. They are ecstatic. They embrace. Their love is again lyricized and dramatized. In the next scene, however, they begin to wonder, "Where have you been all this time?" "Why didn't you find me sooner?"

They argue. Within minutes, the intense ecstasy turns to intense anxiety, anger, and pain. Quickly, we see how their emotional process led to cutoff in the first place.

When the polarity of the emotional intensity that powered the attraction switched, it became a repelling magnetic force. One wonders, does the powerful positive-feelings phase itself somehow set up the situation to induce the negativity? If the tenor and the soprano had allowed their emotional intensity to develop more slowly, less lavishly, would their relationship have fared better?

Mrs. U, who knew very little about her extended family, began to explore the phenomenon of cutoff in it. She found cutoff so prevalent that there were entire branches of her family she did not know existed.[6] The more she learned about her family's emotional process, the more she understood her own tendency to cut off. As she included more people in her family into her life, there was less intensity in her marriage and within herself. Her marriage, which had been okay, but boring, came alive as she herself came alive in her family of origin.

When cutoff occurs, what can be done? As a first step, the pattern must simply be recognized. Often, when one sees the pattern, next steps become clear. Distancing and cutoff may be taking place many times in any given day. But seeing cutoff as a life pattern makes it possible to see the anxiety that accompanies it. That anxiety is grounded in unresolved emotional attachments—the togetherness that develops in the original family—the inability to be a self in relationships.

Working with the togetherness tendency in self—the fusion and the anxiety that promotes it and comes from it at the same time—may be more productive than going at the distance or cutoff pattern that is, really, only a symptom of the underlying togetherness anxiety. Relaxation training and other pursuits (such as hobbies or humor) that lower anxiety can be useful along the way. Any relationship can become overtaxed if the partners routinely bring all their emotional reactivity into it.

As with other relationship patterns, it may be useful to ask: "What is my part in this cutoff?" Better yet, is, "What is my part in the intensity of emotion that led to the cutoff?" Another great question is, "How can I work to lower my intensity so that cutoff will be less inevitable in the future?"

Cutoff can never be changed until someone takes the initiative and begins to move responsibly in the relationship, making meaningful contact. *It doesn't matter who takes the first step.* It only matters that it be taken. But working to bridge cutoffs in one's family of origin carries tremendous personal rewards.

Thinking It Over

The more emotionally intense a relationship, (a symptom of unresolved emotional attachment) the more it is prone to cutoff. But as a way of life, cutoff leads to physical, social (acting out or addictions) or mental/emotional symptoms.

Real Life Research

1. How many cut off branches can you find on your family diagram?

2. Do you or does someone in your family know anyone from any of these branches or how they might be contacted?

3. Are there important cutoffs in recent generations or in your nuclear family that you might be able to bridge?

4. Are there any potential cutoffs brewing now in your family?

5. Is immigration a prominent factor in your family? If so, after the immigration, did the families stay in contact?

6. Do you see cutoff in your workplace? What form(s) does it take?

7.   If you are involved in any of those, are there bridging actions you might take?

8.   Could the concept of cutoff apply to international relations? What would be some examples?

Endnotes

1.   Bowen, Murray, *Family Therapy in Clinical Practice,* Jason Aronson, New York, 1978, p. 382.

2.   Louise Rauseo is studying cutoff in families in the Southwest who have immigrated.

3.   See Titelman, Peter, ed. *Emotional Cutoff,* Hayworth Press, New York, 2003.

4.   Bowen, *op. cit.*, p. 536.

5.   That anxiety can be stepped up at the time of increased anxiety in the system, such as around a "nodal event," i.e., when someone leaves or enters a system.

6.   We all have branches that we know nothing about, owing to cutoffs that occurred many generations back.

OVERFUNCTIONING/
UNDERFUNCTIONING RECIPROCITY

> Each does some adapting to the other and it is usual for each
> to believe he or she gives in more than the other. The one
> who functions for long periods of time in the adaptive position
> gradually loses the ability to function and make decisions for
> self.[1]

Murray Bowen, 1976

Mr. and Mrs. R never went on vacation. They couldn't. Mrs. R's
physical and emotional health were too unpredictable. Often she
didn't feel like doing much of anything. She felt miserable all the
time, but doctors couldn't find the source of her symptoms. When
she wasn't physically ill, she was depressed. She and Mr. R. would
sometimes go to see their grown children, but she never enjoyed
the trips. She was always glad to be home again with access to her
accustomed care system.

Mrs. R worried a great deal about what she would do if her
husband ever left her. She considered that a real possibility since
she knew she must be a very difficult person to be around. Mrs. R
berated herself continually. She said to the therapist: "I know what I
should do. Everyone tells me I should get involved in life, in activities,
or a job. I should diet and lose all this weight. I just don't do any of
it. I can't. I'm not motivated. Doctor, please help me. Please tell me
what to do!"

Mr. R was successful. He could be away from his work whenever
necessary, which was fortunate since Mrs. R needed him at home
a great deal of the time. When he looked back over their lives together, he wondered what had gone wrong. During the earlier years,
when he had been building a business and she was raising their two

children, Mrs. R had seemed to be okay. She had had some small bouts of depression now and then, but they were easily cleared up by prescriptions that her family doctor gave her. Now that they had more time and money, they were able to do and have practically anything they wanted, but Mrs. R was too ill to enjoy life. Mr. R. had tried everything he could think of to help her.

He often gave advice to his wife: "What you need are some interests. Look at me. I'm on the boards of several organizations. I enjoy many friends, many activities. I enjoy my career greatly and I love to travel. We could be traveling more now. There are so many places I'd like to go and people I'd like to see. I want us to do these things together."

He took most of the responsibility for the household and for the relationship. He cooked almost all their meals when they didn't eat out. He did the laundry on the weekends and saw to it they had competent household help. The more he did for her, the sicker she seemed to be. She never took any of his suggestions. That was the part that was hardest to understand. The active approach to life and helping other people had worked so well for him. He knew that if she would try this, it would work for her, too. But she seemed unwilling to do anything for herself—or was she just too sick to try?

Mrs. R, for her part, agreed with everything her husband said. Yet she could not bring herself to attempt any of his suggestions. When she did, to please him, she was more miserable than usual. She spent a lot of time worrying about what would become of her if anything happened to him. She knew she was not the life partner to him she wanted to be. What if he should leave her? When he became impatient with her and all of her complaints, she really worried about that possibility. And yet, year after weary year, nothing ever seemed to change.

Mr. and Mrs. R had created a relationship of overfunctioning/underfunctioning reciprocity, where one person of the pair does quite well in life, standing in contrast to the despair and dysfunction of the other. One is the teller, the other the listener. One is the preacher, the other the congregation. Both partners usually agree that one is doing well and that "the problem" rests solely in the dysfunctional one.

This way of handling relationship fusion, or the exchange of self in a relationship, is often termed the "dysfunctional spouse" posture because of the frequency with which the submissive or adaptive spouse becomes symptomatic. The partners in an overfunctioning/ underfunctioning reciprocity have varying degrees of understanding as to how the relationship itself brings about the dependency and illness of the underfunctioning one. One of the two may see that the relationship contributes to the illness but has no idea how to break the long-standing pattern. While the overfunctioner in this example is male, the roles are just as often the reverse.

Overfunctioning/underfunctioning reciprocity can be diagrammed as follows:

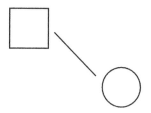

Figure 5.1. Overfunctioning/underfunctioning reciprocity.

Overfunctioners are known for:
- Advice-giving,
- Doing things for others they could do for themselves,
- Worrying about other people,
- Feeling more responsibility for others than is actually needed,
- Knowing what is best for others,
- Talking more than listening,
- Having goals for others that they don't have for themselves,
- Experiencing periodic, sudden "burnout" or severe illness in other forms,

- Taking charge of others' lives,
- Doing well in life, but someone close to them is not.

Underfunctioners, on the other hand:

- Ask for advice when what is needed is to think things out, independently,
- Get others to help when help is not needed,
- Act irresponsibly,
- Listen more than talk,
- Float along without goals,
- Set goals, but don't follow through,
- Become mentally or physically ill frequently,
- May have substance addiction problems,
- Put others in charge of their lives.

Both partners often think of the overfunctioning partner as healthier, more independent and more emotionally mature than the underfunctioning one. Actually this is not the case. The overfunctioner is just as caught in the relationship process as is the underfunctioner. Often overfunctioners, though they may lead productive lives much of the time, may themselves be subject to sudden physical illness of "burnout" because of the overload they carry in being responsible for two (or more) people.

Overfunctioning/underfunctioning may or may not be a total way of life for any individual. In all the relationship postures, there are degrees, and patterns within patterns. The tyrannical boss at work may be underfunctioning in his relationship with his wife at home. Or a couple may be seen to take turns in the two positions, one overfunctioning for awhile, or on some issues, then underfunctioning while the other overfunctions at other times or on other issues.

Therapists often joke, "Every overfunctioner deserves his underfunctioner." It is just as true that every underfunctioner deserves his/her overfunctioner. Each is in a bind. Family systems theory tells us that *each partner in an important relationship is exactly as emotionally mature as the other.* Otherwise the two would not attract. This often comes as quite a shock to the overfunctioner who thinks he or she is the healthy, more adequate, or more talented member of the pair. Actually over-responsibility is exactly as irresponsible as under-responsibility.

The fact of the matter is that the overfunctioner's success in life takes place in the context of a relationship barter that is an effort to make a self out of two. This is to the advantage of the overfunctioner, who gains energy out of the relationship. It makes one feel good to help someone else. So the relationship becomes a source of "cheap energy"[2] for the overfunctioner, who can go quite far on this kind of steam. He or she gains functional self from the other, who loses self into the relationship fusion. Overfunctioners pose relationship problems for others. They are experienced as bossy, arrogant, know-it-alls, and domineering. Underfunctioners, though they contribute self to the overfunctioners, present relationship problems as well. They are felt to be a burden, immature, and irresponsible. Or they may be seen as the victim.

When the partners in this relationship are ready for a more equal relationship, they can find ways to work towards it. Each can work on his or her fifty percent of the relationship. If the overfunctioner will stop overfunctioning (that is, take responsibility for, communicate, and act only for the self) the underfunctioner will (perhaps after an initial flurry) begin to stop underfunctioning to a reciprocal degree. In the same way, the underfunctioning partner can take the initiative for changing self in the relationship. He or she can take more responsibility for self and decisions that affect self, be more active in the relationship, and make self less available to be gobbled up by the self of the other. Implicit in this work is defining self to the other in a way that can be heard. *In short, the underfunctioner can be more of a self in the relationship.*

In any case, when either partner takes the initiative for being responsible for self, and only self, and communicates that to the other, protest can be expected from the other. It may become rather intense, but this reaction will be brief if the initiating one stays on course and steadily continues to take responsibility for changing her or his own contribution to the problem. Following that phase, the partnership can be expected to regroup at a higher level of functioning.

The decision to initiate change brought fear and trembling for Mr. R since most of his life energy in recent memory had been focused on his wife's problems. Once he decided to make a move for self that might indeed have a positive effect on the relationship, he greatly feared divorce or even the death of his wife. Still, he understood that what was needed was for him to stop taking over for her in any area or situation where she could manage by herself. He slowly began to move differently in the relationship.

Mr. R's first action was a nonaction: *he thought carefully about the situation.* He, in coaching, was guided by principles of family systems theory. Thinking about individuality and togetherness forces, he saw that he and Mrs. R were locked in a togetherness pattern that was consuming them both. He convinced himself that, for his part, he needed to find a way to become more of an individual—an individual defined more in terms of himself rather than the needs of others.

Watching for process allowed him to see his part in the problem. He quickly saw that he almost always put consideration of other people ahead of consideration of himself and he often exhausted himself in order to take care of them. Serving other people's needs though, made Mr. R feel good and may have been a factor in his impressive success in the world.

Process watching also enabled Mr. R to become familiar with behaviors in other people that triggered his overfunctioning. If someone asked him for advice, he could see that he was all too ready to give it. If a friend asked for help, he was there whether or not it was in his own or his friend's best interest.

Thinking systems, Mr. R saw both his and his wife's positions clearly. He began to understand how his overfunctioning not only permitted but actually facilitated his wife's illness. Thinking about the family system he grew up in, he saw how he had been an overfunctioner from an early age when he had taken responsibility for the younger children in his family. His mother, a single parent, had been subject to bouts of withdrawal into alcoholism and was often not available. The role of virtual parent to his five younger siblings had continued into his adulthood. His siblings often called him for advice or financial support. They looked to him to organize the family around special occasions. His overfunctioning role was also obvious at work, where he often took on other people's problems as though they were his own.

In order for Mr. R to begin the project of differentiating a self, he had to think about how he could be responsible for himself and for himself only. For the first time in his life, he had to find a way to think of himself more of the time, while he continued to be present and accounted for in his important systems—with his wife, his grown children and their families, his employees, and the family he grew up in.

Mr. R started to define himself to his wife—what he was and was not willing and able to do. He realized, for example, that by automatically supplying answers for his wife, he was implying she could not get them for herself. He made it his goal to refrain from doing things or finding answers for others in his life as well. If people asked for advice, he never gave an opinion until he explored how the asker thought about the question.

In short order, as he let go of the borrowed self he'd been working with for years and began to operate more from only his own self, he experienced mood changes. When other people reacted to his different stance, he noticed a strange temptation to snap back into old patterns. But he realized that his effort to be less in fusions with others would increase his own inner resources. He knew it was a better solution and so he stayed on course.

Mrs. R gradually learned that her husband would not always be available in the ways he formerly had been. This raised her anxiety. Temporarily she became more ill. She became angry. She threatened Mr. R, but he stayed with his plan. Managing the illness more on her own, however, increased her confidence in her coping ability. She allowed herself to do more on her own. She became more of a self.

Eventually she found herself becoming grateful for Mr. R's moves toward more autonomy and told him so. At this point, there was more equality in the relationship and each was functioning better in life in general. As Mrs. R gained more emotional independence, her health slowly improved.

When people, either over- or underfunctioners, are asked who they feel equal to in their systems, the answer is often "no one." People mired in this stance will sometimes feel above or below everyone in their extended families and work places. Teaching oneself to feel and act as an equal in relationships can be a major task.

Several combined circumstances in their growing up triangles may have helped to entrench people in the overfunctioning/underfunctioning position. Sometimes, overfunctioners are oldest children in their families of origin and underfunctioners are youngests. If they were not actually the oldest or the youngest, they may have been the oldest or the youngest in sub groupings of the siblings within their families, so they had to take more or less responsible positions vis-à-vis their siblings, or they may have had a position of responsibility and overfunctioning thrust upon them as youngsters.

Quite frequently, the partners have had parents with similar marital patterns of overfunctioning or underfunctioning. Sometimes they've had parents who, caught in their own family patterns and/or emotional process, relied on them as though they were parents instead of children. And, at times, the pattern was not experienced at all in early years. It may be simply the way immaturity is working itself out in the fusions of this generation. The patterns, as we have seen, are not necessarily learned, they can be innate.

In any case, placing blame is inappropriate. A systems thinker will immediately realize that anyone's parents also had parents of their own who were caught in their own patterns and so on, back through the generations. In Mr. R's case, his underfunctioning mother had been the focus of her hovering mother who had taken care of her beyond an appropriate age. She had thus remained dependent. As an adult, Mr. R's mother found a way to continue her emotionally dependent, underfunctioning pattern through one of her children, Mrs. R.

To begin the work of changing a relationship of overfunctioning/ underfunctioning reciprocity, one need not ask, "How can I change this troublesome partner of mine?" Instead the question is, "What is my contribution to this relationship pattern?" The task becomes one of teaching oneself to be responsible for self and only for self. That means, for the overfunctioner, thinking, planning, and being concerned more of the time with managing self than the other.

It also rules out taking responsibility for doing for someone something he or she can easily do for self. Likewise, the underfunctioner will not ask for help when it is really not needed. The burden of responsibility for one's happiness will not be placed on the other. Rather, responsibility for feeling good or bad, as well as for one's thoughts and behavior, rests solely with the self. There will be, of course, some reactive turmoil whenever one sets out to change one's part of any of the relationship patterns. In most cases, however, the turmoil is short-lived. If solid work on the self is pursued, the relationship eventually finds higher ground as each partner finds, increasingly, over time, a little more emotional maturity.

Thinking It Over

Maintaining equality in relationships is a goal that most of us realize only partially. But when the effort toward an equal posture is carried into family of origin relationships, personal gains become more solid. All relationships benefit from this effort.

Real Life Research

1. Are there times when helping another person is appropriate, and is neither under- nor overfunctioning?

2. How can one tell when help is appropriate and when it would be overfunctioning to give or underfunctioning to accept help?

3. How can one help when appropriate without inducing under-functioning in the other?

4. If overfunctioning is a pattern, how much do the good feelings of helping contribute to keeping the pattern going?

5. Is there another way one could one think about maintaining one's mood?

6. What patterns of over- or underfunctioning do you see in your nuclear family?

7. What patterns do you see in your family of origin?

8. If underfunctioning is a pattern, what steps do you see for yourself as a step up in functioning?

9. What would be some examples of international overfunctioning?

10. What would be some examples of international underfunctioning?

Endnotes

1. Bowen, Murray, *Family Therapy in Clinical Practice*, Jason Aronson, New York, 1978, p. 378.

2. A phrase coined by Andrea Maloney Schara and used in her teaching on this subject.

6

TRIANGLES

The concept of triangles provides a theoretical framework for understanding the microscopic functioning of all emotional systems. . . . A two person emotional system is unstable in that it forms itself into a three-person system or triangle under stress.[1]

Murray Bowen, 1972

It wasn't that Mr. and Mrs. T were not caring parents. On the contrary, they were committed students on the subject of childrearing. In preparation for the birth of their first child, Mrs. T read many books on child care covering both physical and emotional issues. The couple attended several classes on parenting. By any standard, they would be considered nurturing parents. Yet Mrs. T and, to a lesser degree, Mr. T, found themselves worrying a great deal about their children. Both considered being parents the most important job of all in life. But both felt ill-prepared for the task.

Mrs. T's mother had been a worrier and had some major bouts with depression while Mrs. T was growing up. So one of Mrs. T's major concerns was how not to be a worried or depressed mother.

Mr. T, in the early years of their marriage, had had a drinking problem. When his wife threatened to leave him if he didn't stop drinking, he attended Alcoholics Anonymous and quit drinking.

Now, their conversations mostly centered on their first child, eight-year-old Melissa, and her problems. She did not do well in school, even though both her parents were bright and well educated. She had no friends and she had a rather unhappy look on her face most of the time. Mr. and Mrs. T became completely preoccupied with Melissa's problems and general unhappiness. Family outings always included the whole family: both Melissa and six-year-old Bryan. The couple had no dates and they took no vacations without their children. Of course, the more difficulty Melissa experienced, the more her parents worried. The anxiety level in the home continuously rose, as did their daughter's problems.

In their consultation sessions, Mr. and Mrs. T both denied there were any problems in their relationship. Everything between the two of them was fine. Of course, there had been that brief period of Mr. T's drinking early on, but both people minimized it and considered the drinking chapter of their relationship closed. Their concerns about their daughter were what absorbed most of their energy.

The consultant wondered about the relationship between the worrying of the parents and the underfunctioning of the child. As Mrs. T recalled her own emotional reactions to her mother's worries, she began to see how their focus on Melissa might be affecting their daughter. When she saw that, she began to understand what to do.

She made a concerted effort to focus more on their own lives and relationship and less on their daughter. As Mrs. T worried less, Mr. T relaxed more. His anxiety had been triggered by his wife's concern for their daughter. Melissa's response to the lessened focus was positive. In time, her friendships, school achievement, and mood were all on course.

After Melissa began to do better, however, her parents came to sessions with rather graphic details of their own relationship distress. Mr. T found a hundred ways to distance from his wife, putting her in anxious pursuit of him. The more he distanced, the more she pursued. With the focus on their child diminished, the two were able to consider their own relationship functioning.

A two-person relationship is a delicate thing, prone to collapse in several different ways. Triangling—bringing into focus a third person, rather than meeting and resolving the relationship distress of the original twosome—is only one of the many ways primary two-person relationship difficulty can be avoided. The T's created what therapists often refer to as a "child-focused family." Rather than dealing with their own fusion and immaturity, they focused on their daughter. Once the "child focus" was modified, however, the distance in the marriage became evident and available to address.

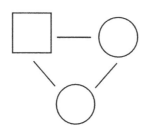

Figure 6.1. Triangling.

Some common manifestations of triangling (yes, the word is used as a verb in Bowen theory) include:

- Talking against the boss, the minister, or the teacher to people other than the boss, the minister, or the teacher,
- Gossiping,
- Having an affair,
- Taking a morbid interest in other people's problems, and
- Thinking more about a child or anyone else than one's own marriage or life.

If partners in a triangled relationship want to be on a more direct, one-to-one basis, they need first to see the triangle. How does it enable the primary partners to avoid dealing with their own unresolved relationship anxiety? When the partners of a triangled relationship take a look at their old patterns, they often find that they themselves experienced overfocus from one or both parents. Many learn that their parents frequently triangled as a means of avoiding their own relationship difficulties.

Mrs. T began to think about how the principles of Bowen family systems theory applied to her own family. She discovered that when Melissa was born, her own individuality had been completely submerged into togetherness with the baby. Her own mother had had a similar experience. Since becoming a mother, she had been so present and available for her children that she had taken no time for herself or for her relationship with her husband. Individuality was sadly lacking in her life. Recognizing this, she was in a position to think about her own life objectives. Out of this examination she gained a clearer definition of where she wanted to go, launched an exploration of career possibilities, and eventually enrolled in a training program. She also worked on relationships with her family of origin and with her husband.

As she began to work on her relationships in her extended family, she could see many distanced relationships as well as several families with an intense child focus. She began to contact relatives from whom she had been cut off for years. That effort facilitated moving differently in her marriage. Just beginning to think about the prior generations in her family decreased the focus on Melissa, a relief to everyone in the family.

Once she could see the problem, Mrs. T looked at the process to see how distance and triangling worked in both her nuclear and extended families. As she gained more understanding about that process, she could see how her own emotional patterns fitted in with those of the family unit. She looked at emotional reactivity—how it traveled and became patterned through the triangles in her family—in as much detail as possible.

Then she began a process of observing her own emotional patterns. She looked at what triggered her to distance and what triggered her to triangle. She examined the emotional intensity needed to set off her patterned behaviors. She could see how, and under what conditions, the distancing tendency resulted in triangling. She began to think of and practice different ways of relating to her husband, keeping the focus on managing her own emotionality better.

Understanding and managing her own reactivity in the context of her family of origin was an important component of her effort to change old patterns. Her initial efforts were at first tentative and stressful. Still, she sought time with her father, mother, and siblings in her efforts to modify her reactions in those triangles.

Mrs. T's older sister had received even more parental focus than Mrs. T had. While growing up, this situation had often triggered anger, frustration, and jealousy in Mrs. T. As she found more effective ways to relate to the people in the triangle that existed between her mother, her sister, and herself, all her old feelings came back. Her efforts to keep her feelings calm while staying in relationship to that triangle—not distancing from it and not triangling again—were monumental. Logic told her she was now an adult and had no reason to be anxious when her mother focused more on her sister than on herself. But the feelings were there nonetheless. In time, she could see herself as the "lucky one" for having received less rather than more focus in her family. She was able to be less emotionally intense in the triangle while staying in open communication with both her mother and her sister. As a result of this effort, she found herself better able to do her part in all her relationships.

It is automatic that when anxiety rises between two people, they turn to a third and include that person in the situation in some way. The triangle is more stable than a two person relationship. Triangles are ubiquitous and automatic in emotional systems. They are considered in Bowen family systems theory to be the molecule or basic building block of any system of people—be it the family, an organization, or even society itself. The goal for all of us is not how to get out of them, however. We are all too much a part of them. It is, rather, managing ourselves better in and through them.

Triangles connect all family members and are almost innumerable in any good-sized family. Triangles connect all the members of the extended family to each other through a series of interlocks. Through further interlocking triangles—in friendships, with societal organizations and agencies—families and organizations connect to each other. In this way, all of society is built upon triangles.

When anxiety is more intense in the family or in society, triangles (like all the relationship patterns) are more apparent. Conversely, when the system under observation is calmer, triangles are less noticeable. The more immature the emotional system, the more intense the triangling will be.

The most common and important triangle is the one between oneself and one's two parents or caregivers at birth and in the early years. However, there are multiple triangles in any family or organization of more than three people. Their specific interlocks are part of what makes the organism of the family unique. All can be addressed, to the benefit of anyone working on self, and, thus, the whole system.

It takes considerable effort to manage oneself in a triangle. One way to think about it is to link the other two together in thought and even in conversation, working for emotional neutrality towards each one.

It is important to become aware of all the forms that triangles take. In everyday life, they turn up in innocent activities, such as asking a third person to settle a disagreement. In churches, workplaces, or social groups, triangles are ever-present. When they become more apparent, we can know the anxiety has ratcheted up for whatever reason.

Once the triangle is seen, it becomes possible to think about managing oneself in it. It is important to ask, "What is my contribution to this pattern?" or, "How am I triangling?" This would be followed by, "How do I neutralize the anxiety when it comes to me?" That is, "How can I become calmer and still communicate with both the other angles, not taking on their anxiety or taking sides?"

There may be no such thing as "detriangling," though the word is used. We are always in triangles and can prepare ourselves to remain a self. Some useful guidelines to managing self in a triangle are:

- Stay in open, calm communication with the other two—don't distance from either.
- Don't take on their anxiety.
- Don't take sides.

- Put them together in thinking and talk. For example, "You two can work this out."
- The preferable position in an intense triangle is the outside one. Be glad when it works out that way.

The B's are another example. They spent endless hours in tense concern over the rebellious behavior of their son Jack. Once Mr. B had decided it was not in anyone's best interest to continue to worry about Jack's actions, his problem was how to get emotionally neutral in the triangle without distancing from either his wife or his son. He made it his policy from then on to find ways of being in calm contact with both people. Mr. B occasionally found ways to let Jack know, without preaching or telling him what to do, more about what guiding principles he would choose if faced with Jack's situations. That is, his talk with his son was guided by his own principles. At the same time, he did not hesitate to define limits and remind Jack what he could expect from his father when his behavior was inappropriate or inconvenient to the rest of the family.

As soon as Mr. B became a little more neutral, the intense "child-focused" triangle became an intense twosome between Mrs. B and Jack. Mr. B then made a new effort, working toward emotional calm for himself whenever intensities arose between his wife and son. If his wife's upsets about Jack would cause Mr. B a great deal of anxiety, he now began to work on merely observing their interactions with as little emotional reactivity as possible.

An acceptance of the other two as together in an emotional intensity enabled him to get some inner calm. He took pains not to distance from them, however. While working to reduce his own intensities, he continued to talk and listen to both, often putting the two of them together in his conversation with one or the other. No matter how anxious Mrs. B became over Jack's behavior, Mr. B calmly listened and responded with his own view of things. He often reiterated his view that he had no doubt that Jack would grow into a mature, responsible adult. He also said he thought that Jack and his mother could work out their differences, but he never offered suggestions or advice as to how they were to do this.

Mr. B allowed himself no more sleepless nights. This was difficult, but he made it his business to concentrate on his own life challenges more than on anyone else's. Gradually, Mrs. B saw the value of this approach. As she began to work more on resolving her own anxiety about their son she was able to think about her own life course more calmly, something she had long postponed. She also started learning to communicate with her son, instead of continually worrying about him. Soon Jack began to emulate his parents in taking a thoughtful interest in his own life direction, seeking a path of more independence and less automatic rebellion.

It would be simplistic to advocate that if you stop worrying about your children, they will automatically have no problems. To be alive is to have problems. But it is certain that children will do better if they don't have their parents over-concern about them added to their ordinary difficulties. Worrying about a child only tightens the fusions that led to the symptoms in the first place.

It is interesting in a child-focused or romantic triangle to speculate as to what the marital pattern would be if there were no triangle. When the focus on the third becomes less intense, another pattern usually shows itself promptly between the original twosome.

Triangles, like the other patterns, are neither good nor bad. They just are, and they are everywhere. As long as there is any immaturity (fusion) in the emotional system, there will be triangles. For that reason, there is no possibility of going to a better way of relating without learning how to manage oneself in and through triangles. As one is less in the emotional fusions, the ability to recognize and manage oneself in triangles improves.

Thinking It Over

Triangles are so important, automatic, and pervasive a part of human groups, that the idea appears in most if not all of the concepts of Bowen family systems theory. They are more stable than a twosome and they make up the microstructure of the family and human society.

Real Life Research

1. What functioning part did you play in your primary triangle (the one between yourself, your father, and your mother)?

2. What other triangles can you think of in your family of origin? How did they operate?

3. Which of these triangles still operate in the same way?

4. What are your goals for self-management in these triangles?

5. What is the most intense triangle you have observed recently?

6. In what intense triangle have you been participating at the moment?

7. Are triangles easily visible at your place of work or study?

8. Have you seen yourself as fortunate to be on the "outside" position of family triangles? Can you manage being on the outside emotionally and still be in contact?

9. How have you been able to "de-triangle" (become more neutral in a triangle)?

10. Do you see triangles on the international scene?

Endnote

1. Bowen, Murray, *Family Therapy in Clinical Practice*, Jason Aronson, New York, 1978, p. 478.

SIBLING POSITION
"IN MY FAMILY, I WAS THE ONE WHO..."

Social relationships are more enduring and successful the more they resemble the earlier and earliest (intrafamilial) social relationships of the persons involved.[1]

Walter Toman, 1961

Dr. Walter Toman's seminal research, summarized in his book *Family Constellation,* was based on the study of 3,000 people. It represents a major scientific advance in the study of the human, putting in place more pieces of the relationship puzzle. His studies led him to conclusions about how personality and relationship profiles are related to sibling position in the family. These findings were eagerly assimilated by Bowen as he was formulating his own theory.

Unlocking much of the chemistry of relationships, Toman's work moved the understanding of personality and relationships light years ahead. Questions surrounding the mysteries of why people were attracted to each other yielded to his probing analysis. So did the question of factors that go into forming romantic, business, and friendship relationships.

Theorists in human behavior have long believed that much of personality is formed early, in the years spent in the family of origin. What has been less clear has been just what those factors are. Though parents are of obvious importance, very little was known about how siblings influenced each other. Dr. Toman's work identified the very order of a person's birth, as well as the mix of genders in a family configuration—all other things being equal—as major determinants of personality characteristics. Sibling position, Dr. Toman found, explained why some relationships require less and some more effort. His research also showed that sibling position frequently has a great deal to do with how two people in a relationship behave toward each other.

His research made it abundantly clear that in order to understand relationships and what part one plays in them, it is useful to understand something about how one's family constellation may have influenced one's personality formation. This knowledge also becomes extremely valuable in efforts to become more understanding and accepting of everyone in any relationship system.

From Toman's sibling position data, distinct "role portraits" of individuals emerge.[2] There are also descriptions of typical relationships into which the different sibling positions combine.[3]

There are eleven possible combinations of the gender/rank mix in families:

- Older brother of brothers,
- Younger brother of brothers,
- Older brother of sisters,
- Younger brother of sisters,
- Older sister of sisters,
- Younger sister of sisters,
- Older sister of brothers,
- Younger sister of brothers,
- Only male,
- Only female, and
- Twins.

Middle children usually spend more time with one sibling in the earliest years (0-6) than the others, and so will take on one of the above positions most often. This will usually depend on whom people are most closely related to in age. The number of years between the various siblings will tend to predict how offspring subgroup in larger families. They may, however, have characteristics of more than one of the positions.

Oldest children will tend, all things being equal, to be somewhat bossy and thus overfunction. A youngest will usually be more the follower. "Onlies" have a star quality about them. It is said that a very large percentage of people on the cover of *Time* magazine are oldests or onlies.

These portraits are to be understood merely as starting points in the important work of developing more self—not as end points or as unchangeable.

Based on sibling position alone, some relationship patterns seem to come up more frequently than would be expected by chance alone. For example, a partnership of oldest siblings, when it gets stuck, often tends toward conflict. An oldest paired with a youngest, if they get into a pattern, may go toward an overfunctioning/underfunctioning reciprocity, with the oldest in the overfunctioning position and the youngest in the underfunctioning one. A pair of youngests can flounder for lack of decision-making capability, each waiting for the other to take the lead. Or at times youngests take turns telling each other what to do.

The most emotionally mature people can form successful liaisons and partnerships with people in any of the sibling positions. In other words, at higher levels of functioning, sibling position becomes less and less relevant to forming and maintaining successful relationships.

Sibling position can be seen as deterministic. However, a person can profitably work to lessen its influence. Given the human capacity for repetition, there will be little chance of surpassing the limiting aspects of sibling position without first understanding it. Pushing against those limiting aspects in one's emotional systems will often tend to automatically heighten the advantages of one's sibling position in both individual and interpersonal functioning.

Functional Positions

Though a concept of Bowen theory is named "sibling position," Bowen did not think about the idea in the same way that Toman did. Bowen theory explains many of the enigmas found in Toman's research. At the same time, Toman's work explain some missing links in Bowen theory as it was developing.

When they read the descriptions created by Toman's research, many people notice that they don't fit, or that they fit only partially. What accounts for the exceptions? For example, some oldest siblings act more like a youngest, with someone else in the lineup taking over as "oldest." How do we explain the people who don't fit the portraits described by Toman?

For one thing, statistical aggregates seldom predict the individual precisely. Further, Bowen theory, with its different way of seeing the family, gives a broader picture in describing other important emotional processes at play along with sibling position. For the most part, they are automatic and out of awareness. In the family, several processes other than sibling position work together to press us into a position that fits into the emotional unity of the group. These processes are to be found in the other ideas of Bowen family systems theory. All the concepts play a part in the totality of personality, but two are especially important. In a concept known as "family projection process," the family focuses on each child differently both qualitatively and quantitatively, projecting anxiety and immaturity. In this way, some children turn out more emotionally mature than others.[4]

Also working to affect personality is the concept of multigenerational transmission process. It is the story of the family projection process going through the generations. By means of it, some lines are increasing in maturity while others are regressing over time.

Both of these processes, together with sibling position as described by Toman work together to form each personality—and with all the processes described by Bowen to create the organism called the family. How the family anxiety and immaturity plays out is unique to each person in the family. None of this is in awareness, but it is part of the automatic reactivity in any relationship system. Some of the factors involved in how it plays out are:
- The level of family anxiety at the time of the birth of a child,
- Stressors on the family at crucial times in development,
- Watershed events in the generations such as a holocaust or immigration, and
- Patterns of cutoff or conflict carried through the generations.

Many people, with a little reflection, are able to fill in the blank: "In my family, I was the one who . . . "

Some functional positions that therapists notice include:

- The "good one" in the family may have been needed by the family after a particularly trying sibling. The child can grow up to be an overfunctioner or an underfunctioner in relationships. But they are liked and appreciated in systems wherever they go.
- The "rebel" may be reacting to limit-setting, to conflicted parents, or to inconsistent limits. They grow up to be conflicted in relationships. They may also be prone to cut off.
- The "sick one" may have had symptoms throughout life and has often been the object of an intense child focus. As an adult this person will be vulnerable to under-functioning.
- The "caretaker" may have had a virtually or actually absent parent and so was pressed into the parent position early on. This is often the oldest daughter or sometimes the oldest son. They may become overfunctioners in their adult relationships.
- The "family therapist" often is included in intimate family secrets or information that he or she is not ready to handle. They can be used in family triangles and cutoff, such as divorce, to carry information back and forth to parents. Parents may use them to try to help themselves feel better or solve relationship problems. They grow up with unusual sensitivity to relationships and nuances of behavior but may become a bit intrusive in their own relationships.
- The "comic" is an asset to the family because of his or her ability, by humor, to instantly relieve anxiety. So he or she is valued and liked. Bowen, speaking about death, said,

> There are emotional losses, such as the absence of a light-heart-
> ed person who can lighten the mood in a family. A group that
> changes from light-hearted laughter to seriousness becomes a
> different kind of organism.[5]

- If "the comic," as is often the case, is a youngest child, he or she may be at risk for under-functioning in relationships.
- The "star" may achieve in any one of a number of fields—academics, athletics, music or art, for example. These children bring glory to the family and so are supported and catered to. They carry the same aura of accomplishment or knowledge with them into adulthood and are valued and supported in the workplace. They are valued for their skills but often have a difficult time with relationships. In relationships they may overfunction/underfunction by turns.
- The "favored child" can do no wrong in the eyes of either mother or father or both. As adults, too, they are liked wherever they go. The downside they take with them is their tendency to distance in relationships (they both loved and hated the favored position so they often distanced from the limelight of excessive parental favor). There is often conflict around them in their systems, both at home and at work. It may or may not affect them.

This is not an exhaustive list. There may be a great number of these positions that could be described. It is simply illustrative of some of the common ones we see. Each functional position carries with it certain benefits. Each also has its weaknesses. The goal here is to preserve the natural strengths conferred upon one by one's position while finding a way to go beyond its restrictions. In order to do that, it is necessary to understand what the sibling position is like and all the various ways one is still automatically operating out of it. This will necessitate getting outside of oneself and observing one's behavior closely for automatic responses that were developed in early years but may now be inappropriate. Small, day-to-day behaviors are as revealing as any. At the same time, it is helpful to understand one's parents' sibling position, since each parent is an important imprint upon every individual.

For example, Mr. S had a life-long problem of excessive dependence on other people (that is, expecting everyone to take care of him). His wife complained that he, by his passive stances, often pushed her into a dominant position. When he saw how this tendency stemmed from his sibling position as a youngest child in his family of origin, he began to rework his relationships with his brothers and sisters. Instead of expecting them to do things for him and otherwise take responsibility in the relationships, he began to act like more of a responsible self in his relationships with them. For example, he began to initiate contact with each of them more often. He then worked on seeing himself as an equal with each of them. After that, he worked toward feeling equal in their presence. He made similar efforts with his colleague relationships at work. Since his wife was not used to having a self as a partner, there were some conflicts with her in the beginning. This was a gradual process that actually took several years to accomplish, but as his work progressed, he noticed his wife's complaints about him diminishing.

Experiments with behaving differently can begin with questions such as "How would it look and feel to do even small behaviors that are derived from my sibling position differently?" Rehearsing them in one's head before trying them out in the system can be useful.

For example, Dr. M became aware that her frequent confrontations with her oldest son had everything to do with the fact that she and her son were both oldests. As such, both liked to assert rather than listen, both liked to tell people what to do, and both sought to have the last word in conversations. This realization helped her to make a shift in relating to him. She began to understand that if she continued in her bold, frontal "oldest" style in relating to him, he would probably turn out to be either completely compliant or angry and rebellious. Dr. M. needed to find a way to allow and encourage his being a self in the relationship while she continued to be a self—not putting herself into the adaptive, shut down, or underfunctioning position. Managing herself differently, she was able to listen more to what he had to say. She acknowledged his assertions, accepted the "oldest" responsible side of him and yielded more responsibility over to him. She thought of him increasingly as the adult he was becoming.

Of inestimable value to Dr. M in this effort was the work she did on herself in her family of origin. She rethought her relationships with her siblings. As she began to see them more as equals and less as "little" brothers and sisters, those relationships became friendships. Instead of always telling or advising them, she sometimes asked their opinions. More of the time she found a way to simply be there with them. Her work on the negative aspects of her sibling position helped her become a different type of parent. The relationship worked much better. Her relationship with her son lost its angry, confrontational mode. He blossomed into a natural leader. Mother and son began to gain genuine respect for one another.

With practice in relating to one's actual sibling(s) differently and with behaviors and goals in mind, well-set neural patterns gradually give way. First attempts at changing any behavior are always awkward, but with patience comes progress. Interestingly, the gains are seen best in retrospect. Consulting with a family systems-trained coach is essential in nudging one out of accustomed positions and patterns.

Functional position, one type of patterned functioning within the family triangles, illustrates once more the power of early patterns in the self as well as in the system. These patterns are set in place in the course of family living. Understanding these patterns opens possibilities of plotting a course toward transcending their limitations while preserving their strengths.

Thinking It Over

Personality, preferences, relationship tendencies, and even choice of profession may all be influenced by the mix of ages and gender in families and one's own sibling position. They become a starting point for the adult work of managing their weaknesses, while emphasizing their advantages. Relationships benefit from the knowledge as well as from the work on changing the negative aspects.

Real Life Research

1. Complete the sentence, "In my family, I was the one who…" Does the personality portrait of sibling position in Appendix IV [pp. 234-242] fit you?

2. Do the portraits fit for your siblings?

3. Do the portraits fit for your parents?

4. Do you see some of your parents' portraits in yourself?

5. Do you see ways that your sibling position affects your relationships?

6. Are more of your friends of one sibling position than another?

7. How about people you have dated?

8. Your life mate?

9. What are the positive aspects of your functional position?

10. What are its negative aspects? How might you think about modifying these?

Endnotes

1. Toman, Walter, *Family Constellation*, Third Edition, Springer Publishing Co., New York, 1961, pp. 69, 76.

2. See Appendix IV.

3. See Appendix V.

4. See Gilbert, Roberta, *Connecting With Our Children*, Wiley and Sons, New York, 1999.

5. Bowen, Murray, *Family Therapy in Clinical Practice*, Jason Aronson, New York, 1978, p. 325.

FUSIONS: THE RELATIONSHIP CHALLENGE

The over-all concept being described here is that of a specific amount of immaturity . . . to be absorbed within the nuclear family, which is fluid and shifting to some degree, and which increases to a symptomatic level during stress.[1]

Murray Bowen, 1972

Relationship difficulties seem, at least to the clinical consultant, to be the rule in human interactions rather than the exception. The following relationship story line could serve as a plot for many novels. It's also, unfortunately, the bread and butter of the clinician.

Two people meet. They are attracted. They begin to see each other frequently. They talk a great deal, sharing reams of personal history. Their attraction grows into intensely positive feelings generated whenever they are together. After awhile, the feelings are aroused just by the thought of each other.

They fuse, emotionally, two selves into one. A symptom of that fusion is the ability of one person to stimulate, or trigger, the other emotionally. If one is happy, the other is. If one is sad, the other is also. More specifically, if one becomes emotionally intense, the other becomes intense. Sometimes intense elation or sadness in one can trigger anger or frustration in the other. In any case, intensity in one (of whatever coloration) triggers intensity in the other.

Shortly after the initial stage, they notice that negative feelings are sometimes generated. These negative feelings can range from a vague anxiety having something to do with the relationship to extreme feelings of threat, insecurity or jealousy. In the beginning these feelings are brief, although often they seem to take over the relationship fairly rapidly. In time, there is more anxiety than positive feeling.

The two begin to wonder what good the relationship is. They stay together, partly because they are able to generate the good feelings periodically—often enough to give them hope for the future of the relationship. Or, they may stay together because of considerations such as money, religious beliefs, or children. Sometimes the memory of the good feelings or simply the overarching fact of their history binds them.

Often nothing works well enough to keep the relationship intact. So they part.

Having gone through this wearisome cycle several times, some people finally lose faith in the possibility of durable, satisfying relationships. Where does one begin to try to make a better life as one of a couple? That is the pressing question of many, if not most people who seek professional help for personal problems. Clinicians routinely see spouses who have separated from each other but remain as unhappy apart as they were together. They see people who fear being fired if they can't get along with their coworkers better. Or they see parents who become extremely agitated over their relationships with their children. Unfortunately, when faced with relationship problems, most people do not know how to make the fundamental change that is called for. *Usually what people do in a relationship crisis is more of the same thing they have been doing, only more intensely and more anxiously.*

Anxiety impairs the ability to think. When it lowers, people can begin to problem-solve. A thoughtful approach usually reveals that the partners are in a relationship pattern that, though not serving them well, is not new. It may have begun years ago. It may go back to childhood or even to previous generations. What is important is that people begin to see patterns of thoughts, feelings, and behaviors. Once they can see patterns and how they repeat over time, they are in a position to see their own contributions to them.

One's own part of the relationship pattern is the only part that one has the power to change. But just as it takes two to fight, it takes two (or more) to create any of the other relationship patterns. Many times, if one of the persons in a relationship has troublesome physical, mental, or emotional symptoms, these difficulties are often seen as the problem solely of that person. In reality, the symptoms are the expression of anxiety in the relationship and perhaps the whole system. *Each person plays a part in producing the symptoms. But because they form a system, if one person changes his or her contribution to the relationship problem the whole pattern will change.*

It is useful to try to understand as much as one can about the pattern—how it developed and what currently triggers it. But the hard work of changing it is solely an effort of focusing on one's own contribution to it. From the beginning, thinking is required to understand what is going on. Some good questions are: "How do family patterns enter into the present situation?" "What is one's own contribution to perpetuating it?" and "What course of action can be taken to change one's participation in it?" To make a change, someone will need to take the initiative. Practice is required, too. One's own part in relationship patterns can always be learned by watching and listening objectively. The patient practice of trial and error can make a big difference. As one is faithful to that task, the other will be seen to improve their part in the patterns as well.

Repetitions

. . .The reptilian brain is hidebound by precedent.[2]

Another idea important to understanding how humans behave in relationships is the tendency to react emotionally in stereotyped ways. Freud observed the existence and significance of what he called "transference." He believed that certain clichés (they could be ideas, behaviors, attitudes or feelings) got established early in life and subsequently resided in what he thought of as the unconscious mind. He believed that in later life some of these clichés became attached to other clichés with an inappropriate emotional strength.

On this point, the relationship between Freudian and Bowen theory is similar to that between Einstein's and Newton's physics. Rather than completely invalidating Newtonian theory, Einstein incorporated it into a larger and more general theoretical structure. Bowen theory, with its goal of becoming a science of the human, relies more on facts than on presumed structures of the "mind." Though Bowen theory does not completely invalidate Freudian theory, systems thinkers use a broader frame of reference and keep in mind more variables. In this way they are aiming for a more complete and accurate view.

Bowen thought that the phenomenon Freud called transference is present in nature,[3] but he thought about it differently. Bowen theory includes no unconscious mind (a part of the transference phenomenon in Freudian theory). A way of understanding repetitive emotional phenomena, unexplainable by the strength of the trigger, therefore becomes necessary.

Repetitive reactions and behaviors—similar to what is called transference in traditional theory—may be more accurately seen as impressed on the nervous system of the individual early in life, through many repetitions, in the triangles of the family of origin. They are experienced and acted out throughout life—unless and until the individual moves to a level of functioning that affords more choice of response.

MacLean,[4] in his detailed dissections and architectural studies of the brains of higher mammals, realized that the lower portions were strikingly similar, both cellularly and in construction, to the brains of reptiles. He named that portion of the brain "reptilian." It directs instincts such as homing, repetitious behavior, and many other emotional responses. Lorenz[5] studied the imprinting phenomenon that occurs in specific windows of time in which animals are especially vulnerable. For example, when he studied the imprinting phenomenon in geese, he found that if a human instead of a mother goose were first presented to the hatchlings in a crucial time period, the goslings would follow the human instead of their mother. Once imprinted, the response was continued indefinitely.

The phenomenon Freud labeled transference is seen in the human. But because the new theory sees things differently, a different designation, such as *reactive repetition* or simply *repetitions* may be appropriate. From the new perspective, repetitions are *patterned behavior or feeling states, associated with specific triggers, formed in early relationship triangles in the family of origin*. These behavior patterns, dictated by patterns imprinted in early life, need no unconscious to explain them. They are ingrained—by repetition—in the nervous system and in memory and need only their associated memory triggers to reappear. The triggers can be anything, but often consist of a relationship posture that triggers an early reaction to early relationship postures with parents or siblings. Because they are relationship determined, they take the form of the well-known relationship patterns of conflict, distance, cutoff, overfunctioning/underfunctioning reciprocity, or triangling.

A more emotionally mature person has fewer repetition reactions to deal with. The few they have are less intense and are better understood by the person as being rooted in the original relationship system. Better definition between thinking and emotional inner guidance systems enables one to tell the difference between reality and patterned functioning triggered by neural memory. Thus, for the better functioning person, fewer emotional reactions determined by old patterns arise.

Patterns We Live In

What is the difference between these "repetition patterns" and the five relationship patterns (conflict, distance, cutoff, overfunctioning/underfunctioning reciprocity, and triangles) we have just looked at? They are all reactive or automatic—fired by the emotional (limbic and reptilian) centers of the brain. Sibling position, Dr. Toman found, explained why some relationships require less and some more effort. His research also showed that sibling position has a great deal to do with how two people in a relationship behave toward each other. Why not just look at it all as reactivity and let it go at that? That is certainly a possible, and probably for some, a useful approach.

Also, just as we see the five relationship patterns as rooted in relationships, so too are the repetitive reactions. But the strength of a repetition reaction can be disproportionately stronger than the degree of the trigger. Bowen talked about them as follows:

> Special attention goes to defining the system of automatic emotional responses that operate largely out of awareness. They are so numerous that one could probably spend a lifetime and never define all of them. In general, they consist of minor emotional stimuli in one that trigger major emotional responses in the other. The response may involve any of the five senses, but most relate to visual or auditory stimuli. The stimulus may be so repulsive that the responder would do almost anything to avoid it, or so pleasurable that he would work hard to elicit it. Among the negative stimuli are mannerisms, gestures, facial expressions, and tones of voice that can make the other's "flesh crawl." As one example, a husband was so attracted by, and so emotionally dependent on his wife for a certain smile that he spent a sizable segment of his life trying to evoke it, while she was generally turned off by his efforts.[6]

Clearly, to the degree one is carrying around circuits in brain and body physiology that are grounded in past relationships, one is not free to respond to present relationships appropriately. The repetition reaction patterns interfere too much. The more complicated and intense the relationship patterns of early family life, the more they get re-enacted in the present.

Approaching Our Reactivities

Freud and others advocated changing old emotional patterns in the context of the relationship with a therapist. "Analyzing the transference" it was called. During the course of the therapy, one would inevitably react inappropriately to the therapist on the basis of these old patterns. Once a reaction was brought into consciousness and its origins understood as completely as possible, it was thought that the reaction would disappear. The only problem was that often, though understanding of the reactions became fairly complete, the reactions did not necessarily disappear upon their analysis.

Working in the Bowen paradigm, therapists have been given a more effective strategy. If one can make emotional contact with the family of origin where the repetition pattern began, *changing the pattern in that context*, the pattern will, over time, remain fundamentally changed. This is a more difficult assignment than simply thinking things through with a friendly therapist. But clinical experience with both ways of managing emotional reactivity suggests it is far more effective than the old way of working with the reactions solely in the therapist's office, outside the active emotional field where they developed.

When Relationships Go Off Course

> Emotional responsiveness can profoundly affect the course of a relationship.[7]

In *Annie Hall*, Woody Allen says to Diane Keaton: "A relationship is like a shark. It has to constantly move forward or it dies. I think what we got on our hands is a dead shark."

What, indeed do we have on our hands when a relationship goes off course? For one thing, people have probably become frozen in one or more of the five relationship patterns. And why don't the relationship patterns provide relief from anxiety, since, as we have seen, that is their purpose?

Actually, relationship patterns do provide a certain amount of relief from the anxiety generated in relationships—at least temporarily. In the beginning, before they have become set into patterns, these attempts to relieve anxiety could be called postures. Used briefly, conflict that clears the air or distance that helps people calm down will often reduce anxiety and help the partnership go forward. It is when the postures become entrenched into patterns that they add more anxiety than they resolve. So, used briefly, the postures can be constructive. They are probably a part of all—even high-level—relationships. Practiced over a longer period of time they can develop into patterns, adding more anxiety than they resolve. While patterns do divert attention from the real problem that generated the anxiety in the first place, the partners—traveling the well-worn road of the patterns—do not perceive the growing relationship anxiety that lies underneath. Instead they see their child, the other woman or man, or various conflicted issues as "the problem." Apparently, it is easier for us to focus on another triangled person or on peripheral issues than to see the relationship fusion that exists behind those symptoms. Seeing relationship fusions is as difficult as seeing one's own eyeball.

The real problem is, to some degree, that partners in difficult relationships are "no-selfs." Too much of each self has been absorbed into the relationship. As the examples have illustrated, the selfs have become emotionally "fused" into a conglomerate that is only an imitation of a real self. In this predicament, the partners think, feel, and plan more around the other person than around self. The result is that the self loses confidence, direction, and energy. Anxiety goes up.

People stuck in relationship patterns are often quite aware of how they give up self. For example, if they are asked whether they spend more time thinking about self or about the other, they will readily admit they spend more time thinking about the other. A person who is underfunctioning knows how much he or she adapts in the relationship and can readily tell how they do it. People in triangling patterns can sometimes describe how the difficulty in their primary relationship has led to another relationship focus, the triangle. Conflicted partners are acutely aware of their other-orientation. Any of the patterns are symptoms that lead us to think about the underlying fusion, or loss of self. The patterns are simply symptoms of the fusions.

When so much life energy is taken up with simply managing relationships, very little is left over to pursue any other life direction. There is a definite sense of being off-course.

Part of what makes a new relationship exciting is the fact that neither party has yet donated self into it. They have not taken part in the borrowing and lending that leads to relationship anxiety and patterns. Once self has become lost or gained in a relationship, the problem becomes how to get it back. This is not an easy proposition, but some have made great strides over time. And when people do get some of the self back out of the relationship, staying in contact, the excitement returns.

In finding a way to think about a problem, one takes a large leap toward solving it. If one can mentally step away from the relationship itself and look at it as objectively as possible, patterns will usually be evident. How the pattern raises anxiety becomes apparent almost immediately. Blame is removed and relationship posturing lessened.

What one can learn about oneself, one's beliefs, preferences, and the way one's emotional reactivity gets triggered and is managed all become valuable first steps toward taking back self. Knowledge of the family emotional system one grew up in makes it possible to step beyond it emotionally, while staying in contact with it.

Many people gain a great deal of personal experience with the various patterns by trading one for another. Partners, after switching from conflict into distance, may sometimes try to fool themselves into thinking they have solved the problem. Or overfunctioner/ underfunctioners may trade places with each other several times during the day, thinking they have a more equal relationship in this way. However, switching one pattern for another solves little. This kind of change will not make for a better relationship. For that to occur, self must be taken back and clearly defined, first privately and then to the other(s) on an ongoing basis.

All of this, for most people, will be a lifelong project having more to do with process than with end point. It is the kind of work that catalyzes the living of a life guided by inner direction and motivation.

Thinking It Over

Relationships become uncomfortable, not because we care too little, but because we lose too much of ourselves into them. They become uncomfortable because we, while not meaning to, automatically give or take on too much self. The basic problem is the fusion of which the patterns and repetitive reactions are only symptoms. Under anxiety, or when triggered by others, these patterns and repetitions appear automatically, adding more anxiety to the relationship than they resolve.

Real Life Research

1. What relationships do you find the most demanding?

2. How much of this demand is realistic (a baby needing attention, for example) and how much is simply the extent to which you have lost self into the relationship?

3. Were you in a similar position in your original family?

4. Does the same thing happen in your workplace?

5. What helps to get some of the focus back on self-management?

6. Is focus on self being selfish?

7. What are some common triggers of repetition behavior that you are aware of? How do you react to them?

8. What story from your family of origin comes to mind concerning question 7 (above)?

9. How did this pattern come about in your family of origin?

10. Are there larger issues or life postures you are trapped in such as work, family, or a too small or too large view of self in the world that you would like to re-evaluate?

Endnotes

1. Bowen, Murray, *Family Therapy in Clinical Practice*, Jason Aronson, New York, 1978, p. 477.

2. MacLean, Paul, *A Triune Concept of the Brain and Behavior,* University of Toronto Press, Toronto and Buffalo, 1973, p. 10.

3. Bowen, in personal communication with the author.

4. MacLean, Paul, in lectures given at the American Psychiatric Association.

5. Lorenz, Konrad, *Here I Am, Where are You? The Behavior of the Greylag Goose,* Harper Collins, New York,1992.

6. Bowen, *Family Therapy in Clinical Practice,* Jason Aronson, New York, 1978, p. 249.

7. Bowen, *Ibid.,* p. 250.

Part II

EXTRAORDINARY RELATIONSHIPS

A person to person relationship is one in which two people can relate personally to each other about each other, without talking about others (triangling), and without talking about impersonal "things." Few people can talk personally to anyone for more than a few minutes without increasing anxiety, which results in silences, talking about others, or talking about impersonal things. In its ultimate sense, no one can ever know what a person to person relationship is, since the quality of any relationship can always be improved. On a more practical level, a person to person relationship is between two fairly well differentiated people who can communicate directly, with mature respect for each other, without the complications between people who are less mature.[1]

1. Bowen, Murray, *Family Therapy in Clinical Practice*, Jason Aronson, New York, 1978, p. 540.

RELATIONSHIPS EVERYONE WANTS

All things being equal, the life course of people is determined by the amount of unresolved emotional attachment, the amount of anxiety that comes from it, and the way they deal with this anxiety.[1]

Murray Bowen, 1974

Presently, there is very little in our culture to prepare people to move toward satisfying—let alone extraordinary—relationships. Rather, what is usually described on television, in movies or in novels is an early and intense emotional experience where people base their initial involvement completely on feelings and then guide themselves through the relationship by interpreting these feelings to each other. The intensity normally seen in these cultural representations often leads toward a fiery emotional cutoff. Thus, instead of showing the way toward high-functioning relationships, cultural images mitigate against them.

Stable, satisfying relationships do exist. The best relationships enhance the individuality of the people in them. Yet, relationships usually function to fulfill the togetherness rather than the individuality force. They militate against people being more of a self, demanding they give up self for the relationship. They try to make a self out of two. However, to the extent that relationships are used in an attempt to complete the self, not only will the self remain incomplete (since no other self can complete it) the relationship will most likely founder. The more fusion, the less relationship success.

If it is individuality that makes for excellent relationships, how does the individuality of each partner contribute to excellent relationships?

How does each allow and encourage the other to be a self? What are the elements that go into relationships that work well?

For one thing, complementary sibling positions increase the odds that a relationship will require less effort to run smoothly. These "fortunate fits" don't seem to take a lot of work. To some extent, all people are stuck in their sibling and functioning positions at the time they leave home. Their personality characteristics and reactivity patterns will have been partially determined by where they landed in the constellation of their families of origin and what their patterned emotional experience was in that family. Luckily, although these characteristics may seem to be set for life, with effort their negative aspects can yield, at least to some degree.

Even more important to a well-functioning relationship than sibling position and emotional patterns is one's level of emotional maturity, or level of differentiation. Differentiation is synonymous with individuality. The higher the level of differentiation of self, the more individuality and the less sibling position will be a factor in the success of a relationship. Also, the higher the level of differentiation, the less people are prone to fuse in relationships.

Said another way, given two people with fortuitous sibling positions, the relationship may start out relatively problem free. But whatever immaturity exists in either partner will spill out into it eventually and also into other relationships where the sibling position may not be so fortuitous (such as at work or in child rearing). Those problem areas, as well as the fusion anxiety of the relationship itself, will ultimately create relationship difficulties. In any case, what it takes to improve a relationship is two people working toward a better level of emotional functioning—that is, becoming more and more autonomous selves, in good contact with each other. *The higher the level of functioning of each partner as an individual, the better the relationship works.*

People with low levels of emotional maturity (individuality or differentiation) attract other people with low maturity levels, and people with higher levels attract higher level people. *Theoretically, in order to attract in the first place, they must be at exactly the same level of maturity.* That being the case, it is illogical and impossible to try to attach blame for relationship problems to one or the other partner. Even enemies, it is thought, "deserve each other." What is productive is not blame, but *to look carefully at one's own contribution to the emotional challenges of the relationship.*

Growth of self progresses slowly, and maturity levels change but little over a lifetime. But, happily, *in an important relationship, any change that one person makes will eventually be matched by the other person.* Even a small amount of change affects the relationship drastically.

At higher levels of personal functioning, the ability to see process as it unfolds, as well as one's own part in that process, make it less likely for the relationship to get stuck in patterns. At higher levels of maturity, relationships serve whatever togetherness needs there may be but, since there are fewer togetherness needs, the two function more as a harmonious team. Individuality is not significantly lost in high-level relationships. Rather, in and throughout all the teamwork, two nearly complete individuals exist, each aware both of self and the other, in open communication with each other. That is the ideal.

To move our thinking further toward the kind of relationship we'd all like to have, we will next take a look at the breakthrough in thinking Bowen made. We will go on to examine the individuality/togetherness forces that are so strong in each of us. In the following chapter we will look in more detail at the fascinating concept of differentiation of self, the golden key to better relationships.

Thinking It Over

The great paradox of human relatedness is that the more individuality we possess, the better we do in relationships.

Real Life Research

1. Does it seem counterintuitive to think that moving toward your own individuality would enhance your relationships? (For good

relationships, most of us probably visualize a merger rather than increasing individuation.)

2. What examples in the media have you seen that would work against excellent relationships?

3. How many couples do you know with fortuitous sibling positions?

4. Do you know any couples or workplace relationships whose great teamwork seems to come out of strong individuality?

5. What steps toward individuality (differentiation) might be taken in a significant relationship? (Remember: distance and other patterns are not invited!)

Endnote

1. Bowen, Murray, *Family Therapy in Clinical Practice*, Jason Aronson, New York, 1978, p. 537.

DR. BOWEN'S EXTRAORDINARY WAY
OF THINKING

By 1956 there was evidence that the new theory might eventually elevate psychiatry to the status of the accepted sciences.[1]

Murray Bowen, 1988

Let us backtrack briefly to learn a bit about the development of Bowen family systems theory, this "new way of thinking about human interactions." In the 1950s, many behavioral science researchers wanted to know the cause of the mental illness schizophrenia. This illness typically afflicts young people, leaving them with varying degrees of access to reality. At that time there were financial resources available for research in all branches of science, including the behavioral sciences. A new wing at the National Institutes of Mental Health (NIMH) in Bethesda, Maryland, was designated for psychiatric research.

Dr. Murray Bowen came to the NIMH fresh from many years of training and practice in the stimulating atmosphere of the Menninger Clinic in Topeka, Kansas. Early on during his training and subsequent clinical experience, he realized that the predominant theory in psychiatry, Freudian theory, was based on human subjectivity: what people said about themselves and what they and their analysts interpreted that to mean. He also had long understood that psychiatry as a specialty of medicine was not recognized by other disciplines and specialties as based in scientific evidence.

Bowen believed that the study of the human could be made more objective and brought into the realm of accepted science. He proposed a broader way of thinking about human behavior and a different way of approaching problems. His ideas, if correct, would apply not only to the problem of schizophrenia but to the whole of the human phenomenon. He had the idea that *the basic unit of emotional functioning might not be the individual, as had been assumed, but rather the entire nuclear family.*

Some researchers had postulated that mothers were the cause of schizophrenia through their faulty communication patterns with their offspring. Bowen agreed that many difficulties were rooted in the family system. But early on at NIMH, it became obvious to him that, while the mother and child were two of the principal players, relationship patterns he was seeing involved not only the mother and child but the entire family. In fact, the more he watched, the more he saw that the family was an emotional unit. Schizophrenia was not just a simple cause-and-effect result of the mother's communications or relationship with her child. By the time Bowen left Menninger for the National Institutes of Health he had already formulated most of the theory.[2]

In order to see if his beginning premises held up, whole families were admitted to the NIMH. Bowen and his staff settled in to observe the emotional processes at work in the families. The relationship patterns were not easy to sort out in the beginning. It was as if individuals were emotionally fused with each other. When one person became emotionally intense, another person would react. And these emotional interactions were in constant motion. In time, the team could see recognizable—even predictable—patterns the reactions took. Occasionally, the staff itself was drawn into the intensities.

Moreover, it soon became obvious that even the families of origin of both parents were an important part of the emotional process. They were involved in what Bowen came to see as part of the circuitry of anxiety that passed into successive generations. But in the present generation, large amounts of family immaturity and anxiety seemed to have settled in one member. Though schizophrenia was considered a disease with a possible organic substrate, when seen through the new lens of the family as an emotional unit there was a greater sense of it as a symptom. To some degree, the course of the "illness" was clearly linked to the pervasive family immaturity that expressed itself in a high level of anxiety. The "disease" was really a symptom of the family immaturity and anxiety rooted in the generations of the family relationship system.

Anxiety in the research families reverberated endlessly from person to person and even from generation to generation without resolution. Because of the lack of resolution, the anxiety continued to circuit in perpetual motion.

The traditional view of schizophrenia, with mother as cause (the problem) and child as effect (the sick one) was simpler. But observing entire families made possible a new and much broader perspective. The whole family was involved in the emotional process, even though the emotional reactivity between the mother and child was often the most intense and, therefore, the easiest to identify. Bowen realized that if researchers were to adequately describe the bigger picture they were witnessing they would have to learn to think and talk differently about it. They began to call it, "thinking systems."

They attempted to replace cause-and-effect thinking with systems thinking. They saw parents not as causes but rather receptors and conduits of, as well as contributors to, a much larger "multigenerational emotional process." This process, while enormously complex, could nonetheless be identified and comprehended to some degree. Seeing the positions and interactions in relationships of as many players as possible became the emphasis. This included looking at the whole nuclear family and even generations of the extended family.

Further, the human family was a seen as a natural system. Initially, Bowen looked into several mathematical systems models for understanding the human family, but he concluded that no mathematical system could adequately describe the human relationship system. It could not be reduced to a formula. Rather, *human emotional systems were similar to the social systems of other species.* In other words, for the human family, to "think systems" one must *think natural systems* and see the human as a part of all life.

A Theory about Relationships

So, while its predecessors, Freudian theory and its many derivatives, were concerned with the delineations of ever more refined emotional detail in the life of an individual, the new theory pursued an ever-broadening scope that incorporated the entire relationship system. Understanding as much about the whole group as possible and working for personal change within it became a new way of seeing and working.

Since psychiatry grew out of the need for medicine to do something about mentally ill persons, it was perhaps inevitable that it had developed a symptom-focused point of view. Based in its medical heritage, psychiatry saw emotional and behavioral problems as similar to other illnesses for which a "cause" could be discovered and "cures" effected. There has been some headway using this approach.

But the symptom focus has its limitations. It can obscure the strengths of people and of families. It can limit the observational field so that important factors are not seen. It can settle for improvement of symptoms when much more might be possible.

Ultimately, research of human systems and behavior must widen its scope. It must go beyond illness or pathology. Many new questions have only begun to be asked. For example, questions concerning the following areas are begging for research:

- The variations found in humans,
- Possibilities for becoming the best people can be, and
- How relationships affect symptoms.

Countless other questions await the research of the future.

Bowen, like all scientists, knew that if he were to make valid observations, he must himself try to stay emotionally out of the field of observation. He and his team would have to be, as much as possible, outside of the intense emotional patterns of the families he was observing. So, a great deal of the work had to be done by the team on themselves. When Bowen and his clinical team were more emotionally calm, the family under observation responded in kind. Under these circumstances, everyone in the family made more sense, including the symptomatic child. If, however, Bowen or his researchers reacted emotionally to the anxious intensities of the families, the reactive reverberations began and emotional escalation was inevitable. Symptoms worsened under these conditions. But as staff anxiety subsided, families could start to think through their problems, going towards their own resolution.

Prevailing theoretical language did not adequately describe these observations. So, a new lexicon was developed. Simpler words replaced longer, more cumbersome ones whenever possible

To better understand the complexity, Bowen's team began charting the players on *family diagrams*. These maps recorded important family facts, helping to keep in mind the players, their constellation, and their functioning. They revealed much about family emotional processes and functioning, all of which facilitated thinking systems. Looking at the functioning of several generations—their occupations, incomes, moves, health, educational attainment, reproduction patterns, longevity, marriages, and divorces—contributed to gaining the big picture.

Bowen saw marked differences in the functioning of psychiatrists-in-training who worked on gaining an understanding of their own families' functioning by improving contact with their extended families and those who did not. This pointed to a new direction for therapists for the future. Working on their own functioning within their own family emotional fields became a *sine qua non* for therapists in the new theory.

Choosing families with schizophrenia for the research turned out to be one of those lucky breaks often encountered in scientific work. The heightened intensity of the emotional processes in these families made their patterns easier to see. Indeed, it did appear that the family, and not just the symptomatic individual, was the organism, or the unit, for observation.

As the new lens of systems thinking was trained on families in clinical practice outside the research venue, theoretical observations held up there, too. The emotional processes of those families differed only in degree from the research families. Families, like individuals, showed a great deal of variability. They could be arranged, according to their functioning, on a spectrum, or "scale," with some families doing better and some less well. Some were higher and some lower on the scale.

To date, there is a great amount of clinical experience which corroborates Bowen theory. And there is also a growing body of scientific research. But the research is only at the beginning of the process that leads to eventual acceptance as fact. It does not claim to completely resolve all the complexities of human nature. Nor does it have all the answers for the problems of society. It does, however, provide a framework for expanding understanding in many, if not all, of these areas. Clinical work suggests that as more research becomes available, it will lead to eventual acceptance as fact. At that point, the study of the human will be as much a part of science as any other.

Murray Bowen ultimately developed a comprehensive theory of human behavior. His eight concepts came to be delineated formally as Bowen family systems theory. Taken in its entirety, Bowen theory opens up a vast new vista on human behavior and relationships. Like an electron telescope, it makes older theories seem like looking at the night sky through a knothole.

The eight concepts of Bowen theory are:

- Nuclear Family Emotional System,
- Scale of Differentiation of Self,
- Triangles,
- Cutoff,
- Family Projection Process,
- Multigenerational Transmission Process,
- Sibling Position, and
- Societal Emotional Process.
-

Though there is more to the body of Bowen theory, the eight concepts are the best starting place. (See appendix II for a brief explanation of each concept.) Serious students will find the new lens opens onto a great number of areas, including for example, the meaning and importance of anxiety in human behavior and systems, thinking systems, watching process, the individuality/togetherness balance, and even the problems of society itself. Didactic training will speed up the learning process and refine it. But Bowen theory cannot be comprehended only by reading books on the subject. The guidance of a well-trained, experienced therapist will take the process of applying theory to life even further.

Research in Bowen theory has shown that the theoretical principles apply to any human involved in any important relationship. Though the ideas may be best understood in the family, they are as effective in friendship systems or organizations. Different cultures show the same emotional responses of all humans and mammals. Because of the internal cohesiveness of the theory, study of one concept leads naturally and inevitably to the rest. The focus in this book is on the ideas as they apply to a better understanding of relationships.

Only when one has a broader, more effective way of thinking about relationships is there a chance of improving one's functioning in them. Because all human efforts are profoundly influenced by how we think, it is important to examine how we think about relationships. A broader, more objective and inclusive way of thinking makes it possible to see relationships both as they are and as they could be.

Learning to think differently is not easy. Some describe it as taking off the head and screwing it on in an entirely new way. But if one sees the value in this sort of enterprise, it can be exciting as well as challenging.

Two of the guiding principles in learning to think differently are: systems thinking/watching process, and the individuality/togetherness forces. Both of these principles are basic to learning to think systems, so useful to relationship success. First, we'll look at the system. In the next chapter we'll consider the individuality/togetherness forces and how they influence the self. They permeates all of Bowen family systems theory.

Thinking Systems, Watching Process

> . . . There is a wide discrepancy between what man does and what man says he does.[3]

> Systems thinking . . . is directed at getting beyond cause-and-effect thinking and into a systems view of the human phenomenon.[4]

> Emotional reactiveness in a family, or other group that lives or works together, goes from one family member to another in a chain reaction pattern.[5]

Until now, therapists and researchers who wanted to know more about how human emotions function studied the individual. Other people in a family were of interest only as they related to that individual. No attempt was made to understand the interrelationships in the family or how the family worked as an emotional unit, or system.

Bowen theory postulates that the basic emotional unit is the nuclear family. Seen from that perspective, a person is only a fragment of something much larger than any individual in the family and is incomprehensible without understanding the larger unit.

Thinking Systems

"Thinking systems" involves becoming aware of as much of the total relationship system as possible. This means developing an understanding of who the members of the system are, their functional positions, how they relate to each other, the patterned ways emotions are processed through it, and how it all works together to form a system, an emotional unit. It also involves seeing how the self fits into the total whole.

Thinking systems is more than seeing the many ways a person's parents influenced him or her. Seeing how various family factors relate to and affect the self is cause-and-effect thinking. If, however, one begins to see how one's parents' relationship worked for them, as well as how it affected oneself and how their parents and their parents' parents relationships operated—not to mention how one's brothers and sisters, aunts, uncles and cousins fit into the picture, plus how it all fits together to form a living organism—one is beginning to think systems.

Man as a Part of all Nature

Bowen family systems theory postulates that the emotional part of man—all that is automatic—is more like those of other forms of life than it is different from them. Thus, in some fundamental sense, *human relationship systems are a part of all nature*, not separate from it. Therefore, emotions themselves are processed with an orderliness and predictability similar to that found throughout nature. In the past, this idea had been given lip service but theories of human behavior have made little use of it. Rather, the uniqueness of the human was emphasized, with little appreciation shown for our closeness to the rest of the animal kingdom. There has been little understanding of how, within human natural systems, emotionality is an automatic form of connectedness between and among individuals, just as it is in other species.

The Triune Brain

Dr. Paul MacLean's painstaking comparative neuroanatomical studies of "the triune brain"[6] clarified man in his position as part of all nature. MacLean showed that lower functions of the "reptilian" brain (reproduction, homing, and aggression) as well as functions that are anatomically higher in the brain, also known as the "mammalian" brain functions (care and nurturing of the young, audio vocal communication, and play) are also present in the human. The anatomy and functioning of the human's brain and that of higher mammals is almost identical.

The human's cerebral cortex—the thinking, planning, organizing, cognitive part of the nervous system—is unique in nature because of its larger size. But often it is not appreciated how little influence the cerebral cortex may actually exert over emotional reactions. Clinically, in order to change an emotional (or any) pattern, the thinking brain must work hard, sometimes for a long time. In addition, strong emotion overrides logical thought so that, in times of intense threat, information processing or long term planning can become impossible or unreliable.

Actual observations of animal systems by primatologists such as Jane Goodall and Frans de Waal and sociobiologists such as Edward O. Wilson reveal facts about natural systems that indicate that the relationship systems of the human and those of other primates hold a great deal in common. De Waal, in *Chimpanzee Politics,* says,

> If it is hard to explain this . . . social organization without using human terms, it is because we have very similar behind-the-scenes influences in our own society. . . . My knowledge and experience of chimpanzee behavior has led me to look at humans in another light.[7]

Just as ethologists observe animals to learn the facts of their behavior and systems, human family researchers stick to the facts. They ask "what happened, how, when, where, and to whom." They avoid asking "why" since it leads into interpretation and speculation about motivations.

Triangles

The two-person relationship is so unstable that when two people who are important to each other become anxious, frequently they automatically look around for a third person to include. The third person is brought into participation in the anxiety of the original twosome. Thus anxiety flows around the triangle.

In any emotional system a number of triangles, with their attendant anxiety, can be observed. Human emotional systems are built out of triangles. Bowen wrote of triangles:

> A two-person emotional system is unstable in that it forms itself into a three-person system or triangle under stress. A system larger than three persons becomes a series of interlocking triangles.[8]

Triangles are so important in Bowen theory that they merit a concept in the theory. Further, they appear in most of the other formal concepts.

Since, in human systems, triangles impinge upon each other, or interlock, understanding how they work makes the entire emotional system a great deal clearer. One cannot think systems without at least an awareness of the phenomenon of triangles.

The more one can see the triangles in the system the less prone one is to take sides, take things personally, adopt a thoughtless position, or assign blame. The complexity of natural systems is open-ended, allowing for the admission of new data. There is no room for the closed mind or knowing all the answers.

In de Waal's descriptions of chimpanzee behavior in the Arnnhem Zoo, there are fascinating stories of how three males vied for leadership. The long-term leader, "Yeroen," could only be challenged by "Nikki" or "Luit" if they could form a coalition between themselves or with powerful female members of the group.[9] The triangles formed during these anxious power struggles were important and endless.

About Thinking Systems

Although thinking systems is more complex, it affords advantages over cause-and-effect (or individual) thinking. The same situation can appear very different from a systems viewpoint than from the cause-and-effect perspective.

A systems thinker, able to encompass more complexity, can usually cut through nonessentials to the core of an issue. Like the team coach, the musical conductor, or the star athlete who is able to keep in mind the positions of all players at a given time, the systems thinker learns to consider many parts and their relationships with each other individually as well as with the whole. Thinking natural systems unveils emotionality for the complex, automatic, and instinctive part of us that is akin to all life.

The ability to see not only one's own position but also the positions of the others and how they fit together in triangles enables one to conduct one's part of the relationship better. When two people are in a meaningful relationship, they bring to it their contexts in other systems, such as their extended families and their workplaces. If each can better understand the other's systems and his or her contexts in those systems, their viewpoint will, by definition, have enlarged.

People can learn to think systems, but for most it does not come naturally. Yet opportunities for practicing systems thinking are everywhere: at work, at a sporting event, even at a concert. Sometimes, work relationships can be seen more objectively and with greater clarity than can the more primary relationships at home. Taking the next step to see how those relationships affect each other—that is, how relationships fit into the triangles of a larger system—can be intriguing.

When Mr. U, who was addicted to alcohol, tried to understand his relationship with his mother by looking only at that relationship, he made very little progress at getting beyond his lifelong pattern of assigning blame. When he took a look at the triangle composed of himself, his mother, and his father, he could see the patterned flow of anxiety in it. His mother focused on him anxiously because he was the youngest and youngests in her family had not done very well. Wanting to fix things so she would not be anxious, his father became intense, angry at the young Mr. U who seemed to be the "cause" of his mother's anxiety. Mr. U, as he became the focus of his parents' anxiety, assumed a frozen, shut-down posture. By learning to see this for what it was—a reaction to the family flow of anxiety—he found some new options for managing himself. Shortly after he identified patterns of anxiety in his parental triangle, Mr. U. also began to see how that triangle was connected to other triangles in the extended family system, all connected by emotional intensity in fairly predictable patterns. The blame game was over and Mr. U was that much freer to relate differently, at first in his family, and then in all relationships.

Watching Process

In observing family systems, the focus is not only on the architecture of the system (the triangles and how they interlock), but on the actual movement of anxiety within that system of triangles. "Watching for process" means observing how emotions flow and change within and among the individuals and triangles of a relationship system. In an emotional system, emotions flow endlessly from person to person. Sometimes they spill outside the family to other individuals, family units, or even societal agencies.

Most lives are filled with dilemmas demanding answers and problems requiring solutions. As a consequence, most people spend a great deal of time in pursuit of answers and solutions. Relationships also run into dilemmas involving issues, and partners can get lost in this same pursuit for answers. People can become completely absorbed in resolving their differences or seeking ways to make someone behave according to expectations. Although this focus on content is understandable, given the challenges with which life is filled and the automatic nature of that response, there is an alternative way to think about relationship quandaries. If one can focus on and manage emotional process better, the issues become less important and sometimes even resolvable.

An important part of thinking systems is an effort to see emotional process within the system one is observing. Observing the facts—how, when, and under what conditions who does what—will show the functional positions of people. Seeing the emotional process in relationship systems, then, involves watching the inexorable movement of anxiety through the system as the actors play out their togetherness drama. The "why" question is not asked, implying, as it does, motivation. It is usually safer to stay away from asking why people do what they do. Even their own explanations of "why" may be only partly accurate from a systems point of view.

The period of observation may be brief—maybe less than a minute. It doesn't take long to see someone's glance and another's reaction to that glance. Or a process may be observed over years, lifetimes, or even generations, as is often the case when studying one's own family system. Whenever focus can be lifted from the issues, however briefly, a great deal will be learned and better ways of responding become apparent. In other words, *the solution to most relationship problems, especially when we're stuck, has as much to do with how we go about the problem-solving process as it does with the actual content of the so-called problem.*

When watching for process, one goal is to monitor thoughts, feelings, and behavior so that all parts of the process are included. Seeing how people posture themselves toward one another over time also involves seeing how these postures are affected by anxiety, as well as by all the other members of the relationship system. Increases or decreases in anxiety level change the relationship system as its members try to manage their discomfort.

Watching for process is complex but fascinating. It is very different from seeing people as being a certain way, or having certain characteristics or diagnoses. It involves watching for as many parameters and patterns of functioning of the self and others in the system as possible, over as much time as possible. In fact, these categories are all pliable and plastic as relationships change. If one continues to watch emotions moving through a group, staying as emotionally uninvolved as possible, one is already a little "out" of the group emotions. Observing thoughts, feelings, and behavior as they move in a group of related people and even within the self, one can often see repetitions. For example, if every time one's own anxiety rises one becomes critical, then a tendency to criticize can be used as a marker of intensifying anxiety. This enhances one's ability to watch for the process behind the anxiety so that it can be managed better.

Mrs. A became aware of a family pattern that was as old as she could remember when she forced herself—after a long-standing cut-off—to visit her parents' home. At the dinner table, Mrs. A's father invariably found something to criticize about her mother. Her mother then look depressed. Predictably, Mrs. A would jump in and defend her mother in some way. After learning all this by simply remaining emotionally quiet and observing, Mrs. A was able to sit through a family dinner without criticizing or defending anyone, or cutting off, seeing all this instead as their problem.

The ability to watch for process implies and promotes competence in the management of one's emotions. *Watching is itself a calming behavior.* It requires maintaining the detached focus of the scientist, for the moment one's emotions intensify, one sees less clearly. Self-discipline is needed to observe emotional process without becoming emotionally aroused. Like any new skill, the more one works at it, the easier it becomes. In time, as the ability to see process as well as issues improves, one is less controlled by emotional process of the system and it becomes possible to choose one's emotional state more of the time. That is part of what it takes to get to better relationship functioning.

Thinking It Over

We are all a part of something much larger than ourselves—a web of relationships called the family. Indeed, to some degree, we are a part of all life in the way we function emotionally.

Real Life Research

1. Make a family diagram of as many of your generations as you know.

2. Connect with your oldest family members to discover more family facts. Add them to the diagram.

3. Write or record the stories the elders tell you about the people in your family.

4. Who on the diagram might qualify as the lowest and the highest functioning family members?

5. What plans could you make to try to develop more relationships in the generations of your family?

6. As you think about becoming an observer, what useful mental image comes to mind (e.g., riding in a space satellite, Jane Goodall in the forest, putting on a lab coat)?

7. Think of a time when emotions passed around a group you were a part of. Were you able to "stay out" to some degree without distancing?

8. If not, what could you do differently next time you get the opportunity?

9. In the last group intensity you experienced, what were the "issues?" Were these so-called issues really what was triggering the anxiety, or were they just added to it? What do you think the real trigger might have been?

10. Make a diagram of the group in question 9, or several diagrams, if needed, to show the emotional process as it occurred over time. Did the group get to resolution?

Endnotes

1. Bowen, Murray, in Kerr Michael E. and Murray Bowen, *Family Evaluation*, W. W. Norton, New York, 1988, p. 345.

2. According to lectures given by Bowen in the 1980s.

3. Bowen, Murray, *Family Therapy in Clinical Practice*, Jason Aronson, New York, 1978, p. 419.

4. *Ibid.*, p. 420.

5. *Ibid.*, p. 420.

6. MacLean, Paul, *A Triune Concept of Brain and Behavior*, University of Toronto Press, Toronto and Buffalo, 1973.

7. de Waal, Frans, *Chimpanzee Politics*, Johns Hopkins Press, Baltimore, 1982, pp. 211, 212.

8. Bowen, *op. cit.*, p. 478.

9. de Waal, *op. cit.*, Ch 2. The entire book is replete with fascinating descriptions of triangles in primate systems.

THE INDIVIDUALITY AND
TOGETHERNESS FORCES

The theory postulates two opposing basic life forces. One is a built-in life growth force toward individuality and the differentiation of a separate "self," and the other an equally intense emotional closeness.[1]

Murray Bowen, 1973

One of the most fundamental features of being human is the struggle that arises out of the need to strike a balance between two basic urges—the drive towards being an individual who is alone and autonomous, and the drive towards being together in relationships with others. Ideally these two tendencies are experienced in a fulfilling balance. More often, however, they are felt as an unremitting tension. This tension is always there in all of us, and accounts for a great deal of the innate difficulty we all experience in relationships.

The togetherness force urges us toward others, toward attachment, affiliation, and approval. It is an emotional process among individuals in which both anxiety and self are transferred. In this transfer we lose or gain self at the expense of our own individuality. As people trade self with each other, they attach in relationships by "fusions." These fusions of selves are the emotional glue that forms the group into an emotional unit. It is seen clearly in other species.

In higher mammals, anxiety ripples instantaneously through any herd when there is a threat of danger. As anxiety passes through, all the individuals draw closer together. These phenomenon identify the herd as an emotional unit and are probably as old as life itself. Indeed, there may be a togetherness force that works to direct all aggregates of living cells, even a coral reef.

The individuality force, on the other hand, pushes toward defining oneself as separate from others. It propels one toward adopting individual beliefs, reasoning out choices and personal autonomy. This work of building a self, with its beliefs, goals, and boundaries that are distinct from those of other people, begins early in life and ideally continues throughout. The individuality force is ever present in all of us and represents boundaries that are non-negotiable in our personal relationships.

In humans, the togetherness force finds expression in companionship, family, and society itself. As anxiety intensifies so does the togetherness force, and people draw closer together when they are anxious. Further, in an emotional unit, as anxiety goes up it moves around and between the individuals in the unit. As one gives it up, another takes it on. This can happen in the child-focused triangle or in an overfunctioning/underfunctioning relationship. When anxious energy is transferred in that way, one feels better and does better, but another—a more anxious one—does worse. When two people focus on each other, as in conflict, they both lose and gain self at different times, depending on how the conflict turns out. In distancing they both lose self as energy is absorbed into the relationship that is distanced. In that way *something of each self is exchanged between them.* One person gains and the other person loses self as the one viewed as having a problem is focused on by both. In an emotional system, whatever affects one affects all.

The togetherness force creates *fusion* between people. And movement of psychic energy, or anxiety, is characteristic of fusion in relationships. To the degree that fusions exist in relationships, selves are increased, diminished, or impinged. If anxiety is taken on, self is diminished. If anxiety is off-loaded, self is increased. Fusion, or togetherness, is automatic at lower levels of emotional maturity or at any level when anxiety is running high. While fusion alleviates the anxiety of being alone in the face of outside danger, *it produces discomfort of its own.* When fusions become intense enough, they can interfere with development or push people in the direction of relationship aversion.

The individuality and togetherness forces generate a tension that is a natural and inevitable fact of human life. Their intense and opposing qualities mean that constant and concerted effort is required to keep life on track.

Is there a proper ratio of individuality to togetherness? People at high levels of individuality or emotional maturity are able to enjoy relationships, with little need to complete themselves in, or route their anxiety through, another person. Relationships without togetherness are comfortable and run smoothly. That is not to say that togetherness is a bad thing. Though it may not feel good, togetherness is an automatic emotional reaction, neither good nor bad, but simply a fact of life.

A more emotionally mature individual finds it easier to manage the individuality/togetherness forces because there is less automatic pull into the togetherness. This person is a more emotionally complete self with less need for attachment to another person. Life is more comfortable, whether he or she is in a relationship or not. The more emotionally mature person has a greater amount of self with which to negotiate the problems of life, especially those having to do with relationships.

At lower levels of emotional maturity, people tend to seek comfort in the togetherness of relationships. They seek someone (or several people) to complete the lack of self they experience in life. They try to make a self out of two (or more) selves.[2]

Married people sometimes long for the opportunities for fulfillment of the individuality force they imagine are present in the single life. Single people may long, just as intensely, for the fulfillment of the urge toward togetherness that marriage provides. One's individuality, however, can best be developed and tested in the dual crucibles of times alone as well as being together with others in relationships.

The emotional intensity of a significant relationship acts to stimulate the drive toward togetherness. As each partner finds personal meaning in the relationship, the togetherness force becomes more intense, as though some sort of gravitational force were operating. The thinking, feeling, and behavior of each becomes other-oriented. The relationship becomes a distraction from individuality (acting, feeling, thinking as a separate self), and focus on self is obscured. Once the primary focus is off self and on someone else, life direction veers toward togetherness.

The pull toward togetherness increases at times of intensified anxiety in the emotional system. It is not uncommon for a marriage to take place soon after a death of an emotionally significant person in a family. Individuality is difficult to maintain and may become easily lost to togetherness. For example, what happens to the ideals of a supposedly solid individual socializing with his colleagues on a coffee break? In the strong pull of group togetherness, his individuality-based principles can be easily surrendered during the telling of a racist joke or gossip.

The state of being alone should not be mistaken for individuality. A well-defined self can be alone comfortably. But aloneness as a lifestyle can easily be a reaction to the intensity of the togetherness fusions of relationships.

Togetherness is a function of the extent to which one is not a whole separate self, and the corollary of that idea, the need to complete a self through relationship with another person. These "needs" for emotional attachment (togetherness) can take many forms.

Attempts to form a self out of two might look like the embattled C family, where each tried to get the other to change into what they think is needed. Each is preoccupied with the deficiencies of the other and neither is focused on the self. Another form of togetherness is lived out by the D's, who fuse two selves into one and then experience allergy to closeness in their relationship to the exact degree of their fusion. The O's togetherness pattern plays out in one of them gaining self in the relationship, while the other loses self into an adaptive position by becoming physically ill. Mr. and Mrs. T focus on a third person instead of dealing directly with their relationship anxiety, illustrating yet another form taken by togetherness. How togetherness plays out is really the story of any life, since all people experience varying amounts of this force which is constantly present, though it fluctuates in degree depending upon the amount of anxiety in the emotional field at any given time.

Do the individuality/togetherness forces play out in other, nonfamily groups? Most groups trade self among the individuals and over time. They develop relationship patterns that become locked into place, in the same way families do. Polarized factions often develop out of interlocked triangles, as people become less able to think for themselves. Instead, locked into the triangles of the system, they automatically adopt the views of others ("groupthink"). When anxiety runs high, the group makes emotionally-based decisions that often amount to nothing more than taking sides. The decisions are not thought through with logic and the facts of the situation in mind. Unfortunately, decisions that are not well thought through stand less chance of being sound over the long term.

By contrast, a group of people, all at high levels of individuality, with less of the togetherness pull, would not be a group at all, at least not in the usual sense. In a high-level group, or collection of individuals each individual would base his or her thinking and behavior on principle. Each would have an ability to think clearly and calmly to solve problems and each would define and communicate ideas of his or her own when appropriate. In the ideal group, cooperation, although present, would not be based on giving up self. It would be based on thoughtful examination of issues as they relate to principles. Each self would stay thoughtfully in open relationship to other members of the group.

The positions of leader and follower, in a group of high functioning individuals, would be less of an issue than is often the case. Each person would act responsibly for self as well as for the life and welfare of the group, making contributions as the abilities of each member dictated. Different people might assume leadership roles at different times for different purposes without threatening others or competing with them. Perhaps this sounds like utopia. But, as people increasingly work on pushing their personal functioning up to higher and higher levels, this kind of interaction among individuals is more apparent.

The central dilemma in managing individuality/togetherness forces is how to keep the focus on one's own life and direction but still stay in open, clear communication with others. In other words, how can one be the best one can be and still be in contact with important others who have that same goal?

In the next chapter we will take a look at that key idea, describing individuality in more detail than ever before, to see how it promotes better relationships and overall life functioning.

Thinking It Over

The dual forces of individuality and togetherness, present in differing ratios in all of us, mean that there is a built-in tension within all of us that we need to understand and manage.

Real Life Research

1. When have you been most aware of the opposite pulls of the individuality and togetherness forces in your own life?

2. Can you think of an example when the two forces came into open conflict for you?

3. How did your family of origin promote togetherness?

4. How did it promote individuality?

5. How do/will you try to promote individuality in your children, nieces, or nephews?

6. How did/does your family deal with disagreements?

7. How did/do they deal with people who did things differently than the rest of the family?

Endnotes

1. Bowen, Murray, *Family Therapy in Clinical Practice*, Jason Aronson, New York, 1978, p. 424.
2. Papero, Daniel V., *Bowen Family Systems Theory*, Allyn and Bacon, Boston, 1990, p. 51.

THE SELF IN RELATIONSHIP

A graduated scale . . . leads from the total lack of self (undifferentiation), at the lower end, to the total presence of self (differentiation), at the upper end. . . . It is an amazingly accurate concept that describes the factual way an individual is different from all others in the relationship system. . . . On a descriptive level, it is a relationship phenomenon between self and important others.[1]

Murray Bowen, 1988

If what it takes to have great relationships is to move a bit out of one's tendency to emotionally fuse with others, towards more emotional autonomy and maturity, what exactly does that mean?

One of the most important ideas toward improving relationships is that of differentiation of self. Simply put, the concept states that *individuals vary in their ability to adapt—that is, to cope with the demands of life, to stay out of fusions in relationships, to separate their thinking and feeling functions, and to have and reach their goals.*

The Scale of Differentiation of Self

People range from high levels of differentiation to low levels, on a hypothetical scale, depending on how much basic self is present. Basic, or "solid self," is the part of self that is nonnegotiable in relationships. Basic self is "differentiated" or separated, from the emotional system of one's family while growing up and is present to different degrees in people and families. Differentiation develops in the context of mother/father/child/family togetherness. The degree to which it is set even in infancy by the family system may be considerable. Differing degrees of competency have been observed even among newborns. In general it is thought that one's highest level of differentiation is set within the family system sometime before leaving home.

At higher levels of differentiation, more basic self is present and there is less tendency for attachment of self to others. This is because one has more completely separated emotionally from the original family emotional system and its fusions. Lack of emotional attachment does not imply emotional distance from family members. On the contrary, it is the emotional fusions that are uncomfortable, creating anxiety and distance in relationships. With less emotional attachment, we see the development of more openness, equanimity, and ability to cooperate as well as to stand by principles.

People reach adulthood with differing amounts of basic self. This means that greater or lesser amounts of self were formed in their original families, because of more or less separation of self from the other selves in the family. Thus, at lower levels, the self is incompletely differentiated. Other family members were functioning for, dictating to, or worrying about them—completing them— and they were not totally functioning for self. They were fused into the relationships of the system.

In other words, the amount of basic self is inversely proportional to our tendency to fuse into relationships. *In adulthood we try to complete or compensate for whatever lack of self we end up with by fusing into relationships with others to the same degree we did in our original families.* Our trying to complete ourselves in this way, through attachment with others, is automatic and outside of awareness (see figure 12.1).

Differentiation In Other Species

Variation among individuals for adaptation is also seen in other species. Jane Goodall's observations of chimpanzees at Gombe Stream encompass a wide range of adaptation. Her studies show that some are more competent than others in socially interactions, in rearing their young, and in simply surviving,. This variation can be seen as

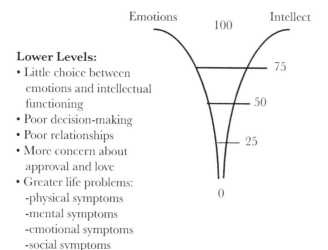

Higher Levels:
- Greater choice between emotions and intellectual functioning
- Better decision-making
- Better relationships
- Less concern for approval and love
- Fewer life problems:
  -physical symptoms
  -mental symptoms
  -emotional symptoms
  -social symptoms

Emotions   100   Intellect

Lower Levels:
- Little choice between emotions and intellectual functioning
- Poor decision-making
- Poor relationships
- More concern about approval and love
- Greater life problems:
  -physical symptoms
  -mental symptoms
  -emotional symptoms
  -social symptoms

75

50

25

0

Figure 12.1. Differentiation of Self.

different levels of differentiation in that species. One chimp, "Flint," and his mother, "Flo," were so emotionally attached that Flint's infancy was protracted and he never separated from his mother, staying very near her. When his mother became old and died, Flint, although he was eight-and-a-half years old (an age of independence for most chimps), "fell into a state of grief and depression."[2] He died three and a half weeks after her death in the same spot where she had died.

Sometimes relationships represent an attempt to complete the self in the same way it was completed in the original family system. Early patterns may repeat or they may be reacted to and avoided. For example, if primary relationships were filled with conflict there may be a tendency to complete the self as an adult by seeking out conflicted relationships. On the other hand, such a person may be averse to conflict and try to keep peace at any price in adult relationships. Paradoxically, a person may exhibit both tendencies.

Human beings attempt to complete the self in relationships to the degree that the self is incomplete. At the same time, others in their system will also be aiming for self-completion. The mutual effort to make a complete self out of two undifferentiated selves results in a new, adult fusion of selves. This is based on the need for attachment or togetherness that was not resolved in the original family.

Fusions, which attempt to pacify the togetherness force, carry with them anxiety of their own, intensifying the relationship. But, if one has developed a more substantial basic self, there is less a tendency to compensate for emotional immaturity through fusing with another self. (See fig. 12. 2) Thus, *better relationships are a consequence of a better degree of differentiation of self.*

Basic Self

The basic self (the differentiated part of us) is guided by its carefully thought-through principles. These are organized in the cerebral cortex through processes of fact-finding, observation, reason, judgment, and logic. Though there may be rudiments of these functions in other species, they reach their greatest development in *Homo sapiens.*

At higher levels of differentiation, people have more choice about whether to follow the guidance of thinking and the intellect or that of emotions and feelings. They are better able to separate these two functions when necessary. At lower levels of differentiation, the intellectual and emotional functions are fused, allowing little or no

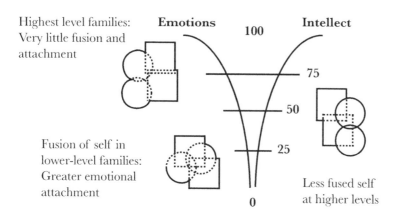

Figure 12.2. Attachment of selves at differing levels of differentiation.

choice between the two with the result that the intellect is essentially emotionally driven.

Many physical and mental abilities and aptitudes combine in a unique way in each person. The inner guidance system of basic self, however, plays a major role when it comes to optimizing these qualities. At higher levels of differentiation, internal, well thought-out principles and beliefs guide thinking and behavior. How does this work? For example, an individual might have exceptional musical talent but not believe it. That belief will limit his or her achievement in music. At the same time, someone else with stronger belief in their abilities, might, through very hard work, expand a lesser amount of talent into a distinguished musical career. Guided by principle, a person produces repeated failure or success. Well thought-out beliefs about the self, others, and the world become the guidance system for the best—the differentiated—part of self.

One of the most important functions of the intellect is its ability to modulate and modify emotional reactions when that is desirable. *When active, the intellect, located in the cerebral cortex, inhibits the emotional, anxiety-producing parts of the brain. This is why, with thinking, unwanted aspects of emotion can be calmed.* At higher levels of basic self there is more choice over this process.

The basic self needs no support. It is sure, unshakable, and non-negotiable in relationships. It has definite and impermeable boundaries and is neither given up nor taken on in relationships. The higher the level of differentiation, the greater the amount of basic self out of which one can act. It is impossible to judge a person's level of differentiation unless observations are made over a long time in many different circumstances. Basic level is best judged by looking at an entire lifetime.

Pseudo Self

At all levels of differentiation, people also carry with them greater or lesser amounts of functional or "pseudo"-self. The pseudo self can operate at an apparently higher or lower level than the actual level of basic self. It is dependent largely upon what is going on in the person's relationship world. If relationships are favorable, the functional (pseudo) self may operate well, giving the appearance of a highly differentiated person. Or, one can take on self in an overfunctioning relationship position, giving rise to a better functioning position than would be the case without the relationship. If one is losing self in a relationship, however, and anxiety increases, this same person may exhibit physical or emotional symptoms, or immature behavior, or other problems. So, if one takes on self from a partner, one's functioning level can be quite good. If one loses self, on the other hand, one's functioning becomes impaired by the transaction. In this way, two relationship partners may exhibit different functional levels of self though both are at the same basic level. When they met, they may have looked quite similar in their functioning.

The functional, or pseudo, self has more or less permeable boundaries according to one's basic level of differentiation of self. The higher the differentiation level, the less permeable the boundary. The functional part of self is often negotiated when anxiety in the system rises. Functional or pseudo self is *the part that is given up or taken on in relationship fusions with other equally permeable selves.*

The pseudo self is guided by beliefs or teachings from the family, the culture, or the educational process that were adopted unthinkingly, rather than reasoned out for self.

Neither thinking, decisions, nor behavior originating from the functional or pseudo self is necessarily reliable. A person with proportionately greater functional self has fewer of the benefits of principled inner guidance. He or she tends to repeat patterns from the past and react to emotional environments more intensely. The better developed (or larger) the basic self, the smaller the functional or pseudo self and the less permeable (or more intact) the boundaries are of pseudo self. Conversely, the less developed (or smaller) the basic self, the larger the functional or pseudo self, and the more permeable the boundaries. (See figure 12.3.)

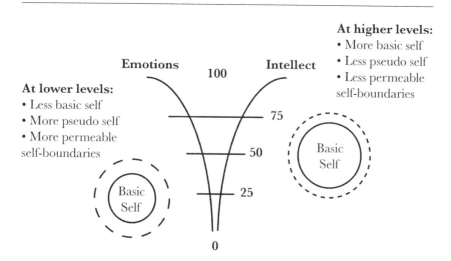

Figure 12.3. Basic self and pseudo self at different levels on the scale of differentiation.[3]

The fact that people at higher levels of differentiation do less trading of pseudo self in relationships does not mean they are less cooperative or altruistic. Rather, at higher levels, there is a greater ability for both. But cooperation or altruism shown by those with more basic self is a thoughtful choice and is guided by principles. It is not an automatic, adaptive, or accommodative response that helps self do better at another's expense. Among less differentiated people, compliance as well as its opposites, arguing and rebellion, are all emotional reactions to the pressure of the group. It is a negotiation of self used to try to hold anxiety at bay.

Since the rational, logical part of the brain does not operate reliably in the presence of strong emotion, people at higher levels of differentiation who possess a better ability to choose between thinking and feeling will manage their lives better. Their ability to make more informed, thoughtful decisions will result in better decisions and coping behaviors. They can calm their emotions in order to think their way through difficult and anxious situations.

Also, the higher the level of differentiation, the less concern there is about being loved and accepted or about the opinions of others. Living is oriented more around principles, making for smoother relationships, especially when some of those well-thought-out principles are about relationships themselves.[4] Relationship concerns do not dictate behavior to the degree they do for those at lower levels. A greater ability to call into play thought-out inner guiding principles when problems arise results in less anxiety about relationships so they work better.

Less differentiated families generate more anxiety, both chronic (coming down through generations) and acute (short term). At higher levels of differentiation of self, there is progressively less anxiety. Highly differentiated persons enjoy a superior ability to calm their emotional states, while the less differentiated person can be immobilized by emotions. The highly differentiated person, able to choose emotional states, can thoroughly enjoy them. At the lower end of the scale, however, feelings and the thinking system are intimately connected (another kind of fusion) and since there is more anxiety to deal with, thinking is anxiety-driven. People at lower levels on the scale of differentiation have difficulty with decision-making because they have less choice between thinking and feeling and more of their choices are emotionally driven. If they are aware of this fact, they may freeze into indecision when a choice must be made, fearing their anxiety will drive them to the wrong option. Also, they may let others make their decisions for them for the same reason. Thus, their decisions can often end up being driven more by relationships than by their own solid thinking or logic.

Their relationships are difficult. Because of their relative lack of self, those at the lower end of the scale of differentiation are in a constant search to form complete a self through fusion with another person. However, *fusion is an uncomfortable state*, so relationship well-being is elusive. They have an inordinate concern over being loved and accepted. This may take the form of excessive worrying about what people think of them, or the opposite—rebelling against accepted behavior and standards. Either position is anchored in an underlying concern about acceptance. Either is evidence of fusion, or undifferentiation.

At the lower levels there is a great deal more anxiety on a daily basis. Some of this is a reaction to outward stresses such as the outcome of bad decisions (acute). Some is chronic. Originally generated from the family emotional system and years of repetitive patterning, it becomes a permanent part of the emotional response repertoire of the individual. Anxiety, though it comes from different sources, is experienced as equally negative. Whether chronic or acute, anxiety, if great enough over enough time, leads eventually to symptoms. People higher on the scale are not immune to symptoms. But it takes more stress to produce the same symptoms in them than in those lower on the scale. Conversely, at lower levels, life can remain in harmony in the absence of stress and given a fortunate relationship. The symptoms of anxiety may be emotional, mental, physical, or social, including addictions or behavioral problems. At the lowest end of the scale, changing the situation is difficult if not impossible.

Most people remain at the level of differentiation they attained at the time they left home. However, adults can raise that level with effort. Thinking out one's principles—fundamental to the development of the basic self—is a project everyone can undertake. Improving the ability to choose between thinking and reacting emotionally may be possible alone, but a coach or consultant (who has been thinking systems longer) can greatly enhance one's efforts. Only a small increment of change is possible after leaving one's original family. *But any change in the level of differentiation makes for a radical difference in functioning in all areas of life, particularly in relationships.*

If one person in a relationship works on getting a little self out of a relationship fusion, the other usually automatically protests the change in various ways at the beginning of this process. However, if the initiating one stays on track with his or her goal of building more basic self (not reacting back), removing functional self from the relationship, and staying in contact with the other, in time the other will adjust and join the first at a higher level of functioning. The two will both now be engaged in the long-term project of differentiating selves. When that happens, the relationship functions better and they both know it.

As the people in a relationship become more differentiated selves, they will have fewer relationship problems. Because of the greater emotional maturity of the two partners, relationship issues, as well as people peripheral to the relationship, are kept in perspective. Communication improves. The relationship is not burdened with issues and emotions that it cannot bear.

The borrowing and lending of self that occurs in patterned relationships is undifferentiation. Thus, *if each person stays on course with the task of working on his or her own differentiation of self, the relationship will improve in time.*

Thinking It Over

Human families show a wide variation in their ability to adapt to all that life presents. And within families, there are great differences in individual abilities to cope. These differences, defined by the *scale of differentiation of self,* determine most of relationship success. Though we have little choice in the hand we are dealt, we do have some in how we play it. Those choices make a great difference in relationships and all of life.

Real Life Research

1.   On your family diagram, do you see a wide range of functioning?

2.   Who in your family of origin functions better and who less well than you?

3.   How clear are you about your guiding principles? Can you begin a list of them?

4.   What possible new principles do you see yourself working out in the future?

5.   What would be a step up for you in functioning in relationships? In other ways?

6.   With whom are you most fused?

7.   How does that show in life?

8.   What logical steps out of the fusion occur?

9.   What are some of the "guiding principles" for your pseudo self (unexamined guidelines that may deserve further consideration)?

10.   What situations bring out anxiety about being liked or loved?

Endnotes

1.   Bowen, Murray, in Kerr, Michael E. and Murray Bowen, *Family Evaluation*, W. W. Norton, New York, 1988, p. 368.

2.   Goodall, Jane, *The Chimpanzees of Gombe*, Harvard University Press, Cambridge, MA, 1986, pp. 103, 204.

3.   This useful diagrammatic way of seeing basic self and pseudo self was conceived and first explained by Kathleen Kerr in the late 1980s at the Bowen Center for the Study of the Family (then Georgetown University Family Center).

4.   For many, the ideas contained in Bowen family systems theory have become guiding principles for relationship success.

EXTRAORDINARY RELATIONSHIPS

The marriage is a functioning partnership. The spouses can enjoy the full range of emotional intimacy without either being de-selfed by the other. They can be autonomous selfs together or alone. . . . The differentiated person is always aware of others and the relationship system around him.[1]

Murray Bowen, 1976

It is safe to assume that a perfect human relationship has never existed. However, while elusive, ideals nevertheless are useful. Clinical experience has underscored the usefulness of clear thinking about the ideal — that is, the best possible — relationship when two people are working for better relationship functioning. Without an idea of what one is working towards, progress is slower. Bowen's clear descriptions of functioning at high levels of differentiation have greatly facilitated functioning for many in relationships. Based on those pictures, a portrait of the ideal relationship becomes possible. *It is an equal, open and separate relationship of two high-level selves.*

A High-Level Relationship

In the best possible relationship there would be a greater degree of individuality and less togetherness. Although relationships fulfill the togetherness force, there is less need for fusion or togetherness at high levels because there is less undifferentiation. So, surprisingly, individuality is more important to the success of relationships. *To the degree that each partner is an individual (emotionally differentiated from the other and from others in general), the relationship will be successful* (See figure 13.1).

Figure 13.1. A separate, equal, and open relationship.[2]

Here are a few of the characteristics of highly differentiated selves and the relationship they would form:

- **Each is responsible for and only for self.** It's not that they don't do things for each other. They may. But doing for the other is not carried to the point of doing the other in, or becoming frozen into the rut of an over-under functioning pattern. Neither is dependent upon the other for happiness or emotional fulfillment. Happiness and emotional fulfillment are instead seen as responsibilities of the self, to be undertaken for the self. Being emotionally responsible also includes managing one's emotions so as not to burden the relationship with them. Emotional responsibility for self means not taking responsibility for the emotions of the other. While the relationship is not without sensitivity, there is no need to take responsibility for the other's emotions, since each is seen by the other as capable of that task.

- **The partners are "in contact."** Relationships take time. The partners are present with one another a sufficient amount of time. They develop an understanding of what is personally meaningful to self and to the other. Neither speaks for the other but for and only for self. Each takes responsibility for defining, interpreting and communicating his or her own thoughts and positions to the other. Conversely, no responsibility is taken for defining or communicating the thinking or positions of the other, since the other is known to be capable and adequate for that.

- **Awareness also marks the high-level relationship.** It arises automatically from increased differentiation of self. Gaining the ability to understand and take responsibility for one's own emotions requires developing an awareness of the emotional/ feeling system that exists within the self. Accurate awareness of the emotions of other people grows out of the immense work of this understanding and taking responsibility for one's own emotions. With time, this awareness is fine-tuned by experiential knowledge of the relationship, within its systems' sets of interlocking triangles. The emotional process of the system becomes predictable. "If I say 'x', I can predict his or her reaction might be 'y'."

Awareness is like the oil that keeps the relationship running smoothly and on course. It is born out of a high degree of understanding of the emotional self, one's own emotional systems, as well as those of the other. An understanding of systems thinking is invaluable.

If there were no patterns operating (only possible if no fusions are present), what would the relationship look like? Of all the characteristics of an ideal relationship, that is, one that exists at the highest level of differentiation of self, three emerge:

- **Separateness** of the partners emotionally (no conflict or distance),
- **Equality** in how they interact as selves (no over or under functioning), and
- **Openness** in communications (no distance or triangles).

Separateness

A more differentiated person can participate freely in the emotional sphere without the fear of becoming too fused with others. He or she also is free to shift to calm, logical reasoning for decisions that govern life.[3]

Partners in a well-functioning relationship lose no self into the relationship because their self-boundaries are intact. Nor do they take part in relationship fusions. They function as autonomous, individual selves in or out of the relationship. Neither relies on the other for emotional support, or expects the relationship to complete a part of the self perceived as lacking. Individuals at high levels of differentiation need no support. Since the self is well developed there is no need for completion. For this reason, it is possible for the selves to retain a separateness not seen in most relationships. That is, each has more choice about whether to respond emotionally to the other's intensities. If two individuals are emotionally separate, the anxiety one of them may experience does not escalate into painful interchanges, nor does it settle into emotional patterns.

In addition to being less emotionally reactive to each other, the partners, if more emotionally separate, will have an ability to choose between emotions and thinking. This makes it possible for one partner to be calm in the face of the other's anxiety. If one of the two can stay calm and logical, anxiety escalates and circuits around the system less.

This also means the relationship itself is not burdened with intense anxiety thrown into it by either partner. Rather, each is able to manage his or her own emotions adequately. After processing his or her own emotions, what each then contributes to the relationship is thoughtful and constructive. If the boundaries of the self were completely intact, relationship patterns would not occur, since trades of self occurs in all the patterns.

What can a close examination of the relationship patterns tell about boundaries?

- In the *conflict* pattern, each person in the relationship is absorbed in projecting blame and criticism on the other. Each invades the other's boundary. If more focus on the self can be gained, the conflict will cease as one starts to manage self differently.
- The *overfunctioning/underfunctioning reciprocity* requires adaptation of one self to the other. In the adaptation process, one gains functional self and one loses it. How does it make one feel to be in the "helping" mode? It gives energy. But it is "cheap energy."[4] That is, the energy is gained only by someone else's loss or contribution of it. In this way of attempting to make a self out of two, one appears to be doing well, but at the expense of the

partner. If boundaries are maintained, self would neither be lost nor gained and so adaptation by one to the other would not happen.

- In the pattern of *distance,* the attempt to make a self out of two or more selves usually starts out as intense closeness. The relationship defines the partners to such a degree that discomfort and eventually aversion to it develops. While distant relationships may appear to have intact boundaries, they do not. The distance is a reaction to the loss of self that is implicit in the fusion. Had boundaries remained intact there would be no need for distance or conflict.

- In *triangling,* unresolved anxiety that develops out of relationship fusion between two people becomes focused on a third. Of course, more intact boundaries would have meant less fusion in the first place and less potential for anxiety to spill out into a triangle. If one can work on one's own boundaries in relationships, triangling, as all the patterns, will be less frequent and less intense.

Separateness of the selves may account for the excitement and pleasure of new relationships. Emotional fusion or relationship patterns have not yet become established, so the new relationship is free of the anxiety created by patterns. It sparkles like fine crystal. If the emotional separateness of selves can be maintained over time, the relationship takes on radiance more like that of a diamond.

Equality

> The basic self is not negotiable in the relationship system in that
> it is not changed by coercion or pressure, or to gain approval, or
> enhance one's stand with others.[5]

Theoretically, since two people are not interested in spending time together unless they are at the same level of differentiation or emotional maturity, a basic equality is present in any partnership. One might wonder, this being the case, how the overfunctioning/underfunctioning posture can occur. The answer is that *even though levels of differentiation are equal, any partnership can have the effect of enhancing the functioning of one of the members, while compromising the functioning of the other. This results from the borrowing and lending of functional self.*

The overfunctioner, by taking on self from another, is just as irresponsible as the underfunctioner, who becomes the sick or dependent one. The overfunctioner takes on pseudo self while the underfunctioner gives it up. The end result is that one does better than the other, in unequal *functioning* postures. But their amount of basic self is the same.

The relationship posture of a better functioning relationship is built upon the equality of the two. It does not have to be worked at, it is just there. That equality is not based on tallying up individual assets. Rather, it is a relationship stance, a posture assumed by the individuals. Each accepts the other as no more and no less talented, responsible, or free. Respect for the other, so often pointed to as essential for relationship success, is based on the equal posture. While equal partners certainly do things for each other and may divide up labor or tasks according to interests and abilities, equality does not include patterned overfunctioning or underfunctioning.

Problems of inequality have much more to do with the partners' functional positions in their original families. That is, how they have functioned for a very long time. It has less to do with gender, education, or social class. And while it is easy to blame the other for the inequality, each partner is actually playing an indispensable part in keeping the pattern alive. Either one, seeing self as equal to the other, can change the situation for better functioning.

When one is ready for an equal relationship, the principles of differentiation, thinking systems, and seeing the process will point the way. To the extent that togetherness is not allowed to undo the individuality of each person, equality is not endangered. As one makes more progress toward becoming a complete and better-differentiated self, equality is less and less an issue in all relationships. There is simply less trading of selves into unequal postures. Keeping a constant focus on emotional process in relationships helps one know when one is beginning to take a posture that is less or more than an equal stance.

Openness

> One of the most effective . . . mechanisms for reducing the
> overall level of anxiety in a family is a relatively "open" re-
> lationship system. . . . An open relationship system, which is
> the opposite of an emotional cutoff, is one in which family
> members have a reasonable degree of emotional contact with
> one another.[6]

A complaint heard frequently from couples seeking professional
help is, "We have a communication problem!" Communication is
an important and obvious part of any relationship. And, because
communication is so noticeable to the people involved, it is often
seen as "the problem." However, to the extent that a relationship
becomes a patterned one, effective communication becomes impossible.
When people work on the postures underlying their communication
problems, communication improves almost automatically. Clearly,
communication is less a problem than a symptom. The problem is
the relationship posture itself.

Relationship postures are different from each other and so
communication within each posture is correspondingly different.
Although communication should not be mistaken for "the problem," a
great deal can be learned about communication by looking at how the
different patterns affect it. Conversely, by examining communication
in a relationship, it's possible to identify the underlying relationship
positions.

Emotional Reactivity, the Simplest Communication

The simplest form of relationship that exists is a feeling-emotional
relationship. This type of relationship, based more on feelings and less
on thought, is seen among animals or young children, where thinking
is less developed. There is a simple give-and-take based mostly on
the emotional/feeling states of the individuals. Many adults have
not progressed far beyond this simple ebb and flow of feelings and

emotions, even though their thinking brain is fully developed. In every relationship, emotions are continuously signaled and received nonverbally. Facial expressions, physical postures, and gestures are constantly being transmitted and understood. Reactivity can thus be instantly stimulated, even though it is not translated into thought or words by either party.

To move a relationship past this simple emotional level, verbal communication is necessary. Thoughtful verbal communication is another important hallmark of high-level relationships. In verbal expression, the emotional separation of the selves is expressed or explained and furthered at the same time. Being more of a self means partly defining that self to the other(s) in a relationship or a relationship system. *Communication at higher levels of differentiation becomes a self-defining give and take of ideas.*

Distant Communications

In relationship patterns, the give and take of ideas between partners is stunted or distorted to such a degree that a pattern is established. In distance patterns, for example, communication is restricted. This is not to say, of course, that the partners are not interacting. There is an emotional arousal between them and interaction occurs. But the interaction is on a reactive basis which serves only to strengthen the fusion, further restricting communication. Of course, it is possible for a distanced couple to appear to be open in communication, talking much but saying nothing really important to each other, carefully avoiding meaningful issues. Often such a couple is unaware of the distance. It is carefully disguised by empty chatter. So, in distancing there is less and less relevant communication. In time, there may be complete cessation of verbal communication long before actual emotional cutoff occurs.

In optimal communication, people talk openly, with relevance and meaning, at least some of the time. What can be learned about optimal communication from the other relationship patterns?

Conflicted Communications

In the conflictual relationship pattern, there is also a great deal of emotional triggering of each by the other. Each projects blame to the other. Because of the intensity of these behaviors, clear-headed thoughtfulness becomes extremely difficult. Rather, each becomes embroiled in frenzied reactivity. Since each is preoccupied with the other, thoughtful focus on self is missing. Blaming, accusative "You…" assertions violate boundaries. Calm, thoughtful "I think…" statements are missing.

Communication of ideas is dependent upon an emotionally calm brain state for reliable thought production. In conflict, there is a great deal of interaction and what might even pass for communication of ideas. But "thinking" is so emotionally based that what is really taking place is the passing back and forth of anxiety, like a ball. No ideas are usually produced that the partners would stand by over time. Therefore, *a second characteristic of optimal communication is that it is nonreactive.*

Triangled Communications

Triangling, whether it is through a child or another adult, effectively stifles the flow of ideas between two people who are significant to each other. Thinking gets generated, but it is about, to, or through the third party. Since the partners make contact primarily around or through the third party, verbal communications are completely taken up with the triangle.

For example, with a symptomatic child, nearly all of the parents' conversations and thinking may be taken up with worry and concern over the child. They give advice and directives to him or her and to each other continually about that one. With a triangled adult, as in an affair, optimal communication between the primary two is impossible because the emotional reactivity prevents thoughtfulness. In addition, because they are not communicating with each other about self or the relationship, they are communicating via someone else. So a third essential of high-level communication is *directness. The partners talk to and with each other about self and the relationship.*

128

Overfunctioning/Underfunctioning Reciprocity

In an overfunctioning/underfunctioning reciprocity, the communications style is one of the most noticeable characteristics and so it may easily be taken as the problem. One of the partners is the "sayer" and the other is the "listener." Verbal communications stay one way for the most part. The overfunctioner takes the part of chief communicator, with communications taking the forms of telling, advising, preaching, teaching, or explaining.

A fourth characteristic of high-level communications, therefore, is *mutuality*. A measure of mutuality might be that each partner speaks and listens about an equal amount of time, over time. Another measure would be the degree to which people can talk to each other while remaining responsible for communicating only their own individual thinking.

The Elements of High-level Communications

From examining the four relationship postures a description of the elements of optimal communication in an emotionally significant relationship can be derived. It is *the direct, mutual, nonreactive, verbal give and take of relevant thinking*.

This kind of communication is the expression of a high-level relationship. It facilitates the attainment of an always better-functioning one. While it is possible to see that communications are symptomatic of the relationship patterns, they also exert an effect of their own upon the relationship, so they are well worth looking at.

Listening is fifty percent of the communication process in an ideal relationship. Listening is an active process. The best listeners seem to have an ability to mentally "get in the skin" of the other, yet keep calm and quiet so as to better understand what is said. They can then quickly get back into their own skin. It is impossible to have high-level communication unless both partners are skilled listeners. It is as difficult to learn to be a good listener as it is to be a clear, direct, nonreactive speaker. (On the average, it probably takes therapists at least a year of training experience to become adequate listeners.)

Extraordinary Relationships

An important part of listening is the ability to separate the anxiety of the speaker from what is being said. Anxiety on the part of the speaker produces interference in the listener. Thus, when speaking, it is important to address the listener in a way that communicates—a way that can be heard. A better communication level is reached if personal anxiety can be processed and calmed before an important conversation is undertaken. Insistence upon continual dumping of anxiety into the relationship is a destructive pattern. Though old theory promoted this by its admonitions to "get your feelings out," very few relationships can withstand it. When one can take responsibility for one's own anxiety and the processing of it, communication will be greatly enhanced.

Storytelling is an excellent way to be heard. It comes naturally to many people. Others must work to become good storytellers. The ability to spin an interesting yarn is a wonderful asset in relationships. Stories, while creative and colorful, can be overused, but they may make a lasting point without de-selfing anyone.

At the highest levels of relationship functioning then, it could be postulated that communication has certain characteristics, growing out of the high level of differentiation of the partners. Here is a partial list:

- **Thinking-based conversation about important subjects.** Because each person is responsible for and is processing his or her own feelings, communications are free of emotionally driven tangentiality—getting off the point. It becomes possible for each to think all the way through a problem or a topic in the presence of the other, with each tracking the thought processes of the other accurately. Less emotional triggering of the two makes this thoughtful tracking possible. Each, under these circumstances, is more able to accurately define and express his or her best thinking on a given subject. The best thinking is guided by the principles of the basic self.
- **Creativity.** When a mutual thinking-through process operates, the thinking of each is stimulated by the thinking of the other.

In this way the partnership exerts a positive influence on the creative process of each. While the best thinking is an independent process at the same time, conversations between two well-defined selves can enhance and cross-fertilize thinking in a beneficial way.

- **Self-definition.** High-level partners can use thinking-based communication as a self-defining process. Explaining one's thoughts to another or accurately hearing the thinking of another can be a rigorous exercise in defining the self. One's stands on issues, ideas, and beliefs all come into clear focus during such a process. Learning to only define self to another in this context will take the "you" out of most communications. Instead, communication will take place from the point of view of "I think ..." or "It seems to me ...".

- **Meaningfulness.** When two people experience each other as separate selves and as equals, they are free to communicate accurately their definitions of self to the other. This includes where they stand on issues. They also are freer to communicate completely, because they are relieved of emotional consequences. With emotional process not an issue, they can trust each other not to overreact emotionally to a given idea. Such communication imparts a sense of meaning to the relationship and to the lives of the partners.

In aspiring to ideal relationships, the three components—emotional separateness, equality, and open communication—for most of us remain goals rather than attainments. The effort to understand each of the three goals separately leads, surprisingly, to the discovery of their great degree of interdependence. The more familiar one becomes with them, the more one realizes the three can scarcely be teased apart.

For example, if one thinks at length about emotional separateness and all its implications, one is inevitably led to equality and open communication. Or, as we have seen, it becomes impossible to consider openness in communication without the ideas of equality and emotional separateness coming in, too. The interdependence is not merely a theoretical phenomenon, it is very practical. Working on one aspect of a relationship improves all aspects of it.

As people work toward differentiation of self, thinking systems, and watching for emotional process while they work, their relationship functioning improves steadily. With some understanding of a theory of relationships and a glimpse of the goal, it becomes possible to take a further step to see what kind or work people need to do to bring theory to life.

Thinking It Over

A high-level relationship—one that has separate boundaries, open communications and is equal—may remain, for most of us, a goal. But even working toward it drastically improves the quality of relationships.

Real Life Research

1. How many open, separate, and equal marriages have you seen?

2. How many workplace relationships of this type have you seen?

3. When you get tripped up, in what area is it?

4. Does that look like a pattern you experienced in your family growing up?

5. What can you learn by looking on your family diagram for high-level relationships?

6. On the international scene, what examples of high-level relationships could be cited?

Endnotes

1. Bowen, Murray, *Family Therapy in Clinical Practice*, Jason Aronson, New York, 1978, p. 370.

2. This diagram was presented to me by Dr. Roberta Holt around 1981 during a coaching session at Georgetown Family Center.

3. Bowen, *op. cit.*, p. 364.

4.   A phrase coined by Andrea Maloney Schara in lectures at the Bowen Center for the Study of the Family in Washington.
5.   Bowen, *op. cit.*, p. 473.
6.   *Ibid.*, p. 537.

Part III

TOWARD BETTER RELATIONSHIPS

A goal in family therapy is to reduce the level of anxiety, to improve the level of responsible open communication within the family, and to reduce the irresponsible, underground communication of secrets and gossip to others.[1]

In my opinion, this process of externalizing the thinking of each spouse in the presence of the other is the epitome of the "magic of family therapy."[2]

No other approach has been as effective as this in producing good long-term results.[3]

1. Bowen, Murray, *Family Therapy in Clinical Practice*, Jason Aronson, New York, 1978, p. 477.
2. *Ibid.*, p. 314.
3. *Ibid.*, p. 316.

TOWARD BETTER RELATIONSHIPS

The goal is . . . to take a microscopic step toward a better level of differentiation, in spite of the togetherness forces that oppose.[1]

Murray Bowen, 1976

For most people, excellence in relationships qualifies as one of the inscrutable problems of the world. This fact may owe to the fact that *what makes for relationship success is two people operating at high levels of differentiation*. Most of us can boast only modest levels. The amount of emotional immaturity we live with carries with it a level of chronic anxiety that, when expressed in relationships, wreaks havoc.

Theoretically, two people are not attracted to each other unless they are on the same level of differentiation. That means that if the relationship doesn't go well, each is contributing his or her fifty percent to the difficulties. However, if either person in a relationship increases his or her own level of basic self differentiation), the other will pull up to the same level. When that happens, the relationship functions better. This process is uneven because partners improve their level of self at different times. Typically, one partner starts the process by being more of a self—improving functioning or taking a stand, for example. The second may protest in some way. Only after the protest does the second pull up to meet the first. But it is virtually impossible to relate closely to a person who is working on differentiating a self and not do the same oneself.

Next, the initiating partner may coast, while the other does a few "pull-ups." Another way of stating this is that in a relationship that is not working well, the fusion has begun to generate anxiety. This is an inherently painful state of affairs where a couple's lack of boundaries means too much self is being traded for comfort. To remedy the situation, one of them must take a responsible stance for self. As one defines boundaries—differentiating a little more self—the other will eventually adjust by joining the first at the new, higher level of differentiation.

Let's take a closer look at the differentiating process in a close relationship. A relationship goes through predictable stages when one person begins to work on differentiating a self out of the togetherness. As Bowen explains:

> The family system is . . . disturbed when any family member moves toward a slightly higher level of differentiation and it will move automatically to restore the family system to its former equilibrium. Thus, any small step toward differentiation is accompanied by a small emotional upheaval in the family system. This pattern is so predictable that absence of an emotional reaction is good evidence that the differentiating effort was not successful. There are three predictable steps in the family reaction to differentiation. They are: (1) "You are wrong" or some version of that; (2) "Change back," which can be communicated in many different ways, and (3) "If you do not, these are the consequences." If the differentiating one can stay on course without defending self or counterattacking, the emotional reaction is usually brief and the other then expresses appreciation in some way.

He continues:

> The clearest examples of the steps in differentiation occur in family psychotherapy with husband and wife. The following is a typical example. One couple in family therapy spent several months on issues about the togetherness in the marriage. They discussed meeting the needs of each other; attaining a warm, loving relationship; the ways each disappointed the other; and the making of joint decisions. They discovered new differences in opinion as the process continued.

Then the husband spent a few weeks thinking about himself, his career, and where he stood on some central issues between him and his wife. His focus on himself stirred an emotional reaction in the wife. Her anxiety episode lasted about a week as she begged him to return to the togetherness and then went into a tearful, angry, emotional attack in which she accused him of being selfish, self-centered, incapable of loving anyone, and an inadequate husband. She was sure the only answer was divorce. He maintained his calm and was able to stay close to her.

The following day, the relationship was calm. At the next therapy session she said to her husband, "I liked what you were doing, but it made me mad. I wanted to control what I was saying but it had to come out. All the time I was watching you, hoping you would not give in. I am so glad you did not let me change you." They were on a new and less intense level of togetherness which was followed by the wife starting on a self-determined course, with the husband then reacting emotionally to her efforts at differentiation.

In this example, the husband's effort represented a small step toward a better level of differentiation. Had he yielded to her demand, or attacked, he would have slipped back to her level. When he held his position, her emotional reaction represented a pull up to his level. This theoretical orientation considers this sequence a basic increase in bilateral differentiation which can never return to the former level. On the new level they both have different attitudes about togetherness and individuality. They say things like, "We are much more separate but we are closer. The old love is gone. I miss it sometimes, but the new love is calmer and better. I know it sounds crazy, but that's how it is."[2]

Bowen's example illustrates that relationship work, paradoxically, is a solitary project—that of growing a self. It is not necessary, important, or even possible to work on the other person. One cannot change another person, though the temptation to try is always strong. Change must come from within the self, for one's own reasons. Differentiation in the other may be stimulated by one's own efforts to differentiate a self, but the other cannot be encouraged, prodded or advised in this respect. The impetus must come solely from within the self.

Many people characterize their relationship as being like a roller coaster; subject to extreme highs, predictably followed by extreme lows (See figure 14.1).

Figure 14.1. Many relationships are characterized by constant predictable rounds of ups and downs.

Any work on differentiation will tend to smooth out the highs and lows. Like a perfect golf swing, a smooth-running relationship takes both mental work and field practice. It doesn't matter who begins the work. The other will usually respond in kind, given time. When anxious, people often respond, "Why do I have to do all the work?" Of course, one has to do all the work on the self, but this is the key to better relationships. It takes two to fuse together, but only one to begin to regain the threads of lost self entangled with the other.

Thinking It Over

What does it take to make a better relationship? Two people living life at a higher level of differentiation. If one starts the process, working only on self, the other comes up to parity very soon. The relationship then will feel different and do better.

Real Life Research

1. Does it seem logical that what would help relationship functioning is getting out of the togetherness?

2. Are there ways you are aware of taking on or giving up self in your important relationships?

3. What would a better level of relationship functioning represent for you?

4. What would be a possible first step toward that goal?

5. Is there a relationship in your extended family in which you could try this out first?

Endnotes

1. Bowen, Murray, *Family Therapy in Clinical Practice*, Jason Aronson, New York, 1978, p. 371.
2. *Ibid.*, p. 496.

GROWING A SELF

The individuality force emerges slowly at first, and it takes very little togetherness force to drive it back underground for fairly long periods.[1]

Murray Bowen, 1975

The best relationships are enjoyed by people with a high level of differentiation of self. Let's review the basics of what that looks like. They have a well-developed basic self. Three other attributes of a well-developed basic self are: (1) well-defined self-boundaries, (2) an ability to choose between thinking and feeling, and (3) a well thought-out set of principles that serve as a guidance system for the basic self.

The inner guidance system of basic self is the part on which motivation is founded and decisions and judgments are based. People at higher levels of differentiation are clear on and comfortable with their beliefs, standards, values, and priorities. This is what makes it possible to live a life based on principle rather than on emotions and relationships. At any given time, they have a fairly clear idea of what they believe, the evidence they used, and the logical process they went through to get there. This makes it possible to live a principled life.

This is not to say that people at high levels might not revise their guiding principles. Guiding principles are not fixed for all time. High-level people remain open to new data and can change or modify their principles based on new information.

A life lived according to the principles of a thought-out inner guidance system has an entirely different quality, course, and outcome than a life lived according to guidance implicitly or explicitly set by the environment (much of which will be inconsistent or contradictory). This makes it possible to say "no" when that becomes appropriate. In other words, the effort toward differentiation frees people from trying to be what they think others want them to be. At the same time, it allows them to remain in open contact with significant others in the emotional system, whether they hold the same beliefs or not.

The guiding principles of well-differentiated individuals make it possible for them to be less concerned about what people think of them, whether or not they are loved, and how they appear to others. As mature adults, they no longer need parents or parental love, so they don't have to spend their lives seeking nurturing from others. This fact alone relieves relationships of a great deal of pressure often put on them.

The well-developed and well-defined boundaries of people at high levels of differentiation mean they are neither borrowers nor lenders of self. Consequently, they do not lose self into their relationships and they do not need to borrow self from someone else in order to function. To determine whether a significant amount of self has been lost into the relationship, an important question becomes, "How much time do I spend thinking about myself and my life course and how much about the other person, the relationship, or a triangled third person?"

Further, emotionally mature people have a well-developed ability to choose between the thinking and feeling systems. The importance of this ability cannot be stressed enough, for when emotions are aroused beyond a certain level, clear, reliable thinking becomes impossible. It is characteristic of the feeling system that feelings are evanescent—they swiftly come and go. If one bases a life course on feelings, that life will be marked by ups and downs, tangents, and lack of direction. If anxious feelings can be calmed at will, productive thoughtfulness will have a chance. Communications in relationships are entirely different for those who can think before they impulsively speak. Decisions are better when people take the time to bring their best thinking to bear. Most of us need all the calm thoughtfulness we can muster in life—both for self and for our relationships.

With an improved ability to choose between the thinking and the feeling systems, one becomes less reactive to the emotions of the other as well as to stressors from outside the relationship. This improved emotional maturity has a very positive effect upon relationships.

Differentiating a Self in One's Own Family

Bowen theory's radical departure from traditional theory and method means that, instead of working on counterproductive tendencies in the therapist's office, one goes right back to the place where they originated—one's family—to do the primary work on self there. Some of his comments about that process follow.

> I believe that the level of differentiation of a person is largely determined by the time he leaves the parental family and he attempts a life of his own. Thereafter, he tends to replicate the lifestyle from the parental family in all future relationships. It is not possible ever to make more than minor changes in one's basic level of self; but from clinical experience I can say it is possible to make slow changes and each small change results in the new "world" of a different lifestyle. As I see it now, the critical stage is passed when the individual can begin to know the difference between emotional functioning and intellectual functioning and when he has developed ways for using the knowledge for solving future problems in a lifelong effort of his own.[2]

> I have suggested to people, "If you can get a one-to-one relationship with each living person in your extended family, it will help you 'grow up' more than anything else you could ever do in life."[3]

> There were comments such as, "Family systems theory is just another theory until you see it work with your own family."[4]

How does one go about becoming one of those people who seems to attract and maintain smooth relationships? That is, how does one go about differentiating more self? If it is true that one's relationships are only as good as one's self-knowledge, understanding ,and self-regulation, then how does one go about improving those?

If there is a high road to improving one's relationships, it is through working toward improving those in one's family of origin. In fact, it appears that only limited improvement of other relationships is possible without working on self in the family of origin. The family one grew up in is the best of all possible places to learn about oneself and make needed changes.

There are many reasons for this. One is that the lack of self (or the tendency to borrow and lend self) exhibited in relationships goes back to those early years spent in that first family. *Whatever amount of self (emotional maturity or differentiation level) one has been able to develop at the time of leaving one's original family is the amount of self carried into adulthood.*

The same process of differentiation was operating in our parents and in their parents before them. The approximate level of self (maturity, individuality, and differentiation) gets passed down from generation to generation. In order to increase personal maturity then, it is most useful to understand the emotional system that exists among the members of one's extended family, by relating to it and by teaching oneself to get out of the emotional patterns reverberating in it. *Understanding and changing the self is best accomplished in the family system in which one grew up.*

The most emotionally influential relationships are those with one's mother and father. Teaching about differentiation of self, Bowen pointed out that it is especially important to establish an individual relationship with each parent. One parent may be the spokesperson and so it may be easier to develop a relationship with that one. As soon as one has become a bit more of a self in the relationship with that parent, it is important to begin the same effort with the other. A goal is to be able to relate to each parent as an open and separate equal. This includes allowing personal issues concerning self or the other to arise, without going into a lot of extraneous issues and without defending, criticizing, or sermonizing.

At family gatherings, it becomes a goal to spend as much individual time with each person as possible. Returning often to the family of origin is an important part of the process, in order to learn what the patterns are and how the family functions emotionally. At the same time, one is learning about one's own postures while there and managing one's self better in the midst of the emotional process. Eventually neutrality becomes possible, "They don't love me" becomes irrelevant, and one can understand from the inside that they were doing the best they could at the time.

Caution is needed. *Many people heard Bowen's idea of going back home but few heard what he said to do when they got there.* Too many go home, make accusations, participate in confrontations, or attempt to do therapy on the family group. Those ill-advised actions only end in more intense family emotional process such as cutoff. In some cases, families have been virtually blown apart by attempts to work on the others instead of the self.

The process becomes a lifelong project for most people who begin it. It often follows several predictable steps that are repeated over and over again. The following is a brief summary of what each step looks like and what may take place over years in the effort to differentiate more self in one's family of origin.

Bridging Cutoff

A useful beginning in such a process is to try to develop a one-to-one relationship with every person in one's family of origin. This effort typically goes back as far on both maternal and paternal sides as one can, allowing one to become aware of and work through the triangles, conflict, distancing, and overfunctioning/underfunctioning patterns that are already in place or that may develop. Where there is cutoff, the goal becomes simply to get back into contact.

Three observable steps to becoming more of a self in one's family of origin are:

- Observing,
- Thinking, planning, and rehearsing in one's head, and
- Doing.

Let's look at each step in detail.

Observing

After making contact, it is useful to step back and just observe the emotional processes and patterned emotional behaviors in the family. Of course, rarely does one stay out of all the family patterns and emotional intensities. We are all very much a part of these, or the work would not be necessary. But, with a thoughtful approach, an understanding of theory, commitment, and with professional coaching, one does become better at "staying out" emotionally while keeping in contact with the individuals of the system.

The best results come from emotional calm and neutrality so that one can see as objectively as possible what emotional patterns occur in the family as well as what triggers them. When they approach their families, people sometimes adopt the calm, objective attitude of a scientist doing research. In this way, one might discover patterns that have been present in the family for generations. With cutoff, for example, the observation phase will help one understand, to some degree, the nature of the reactivity that led to the cutoff in the first place and then kept it in place.

Observation of self in the family patterns is crucial. "What and who triggers me?" and "How do I react to those triggers?" are useful questions to keep in mind.

Thinking, Planning, and Rehearsing

After seeing how emotions are processed in one's family, one is in a better position to look through the lens of Bowen theory and begin to see how it all fits together. Patterns, functioning positions, the importance of sibling positions, and their impact on the family can all be seen. Most important of all, one's own functioning position in the family, and just how one contributes to the passage or absorption of anxiety in the family, becomes apparent.

When these phenomena become clearer, one can make a thoughtful plan to relate to that emotional system in a more mature way. This thoughtful planning is crucial to success. Without it, one will simply continue the same role as always in the family emotional patterns and processes.

Rehearsing

Mentally rehearsing a personal plan for participating differently in relationships can be extremely important. If actors do not overlearn their lines, the double stressors of bright lights and staring audience eyes will make their lines difficult to remember. In the same way, a plan for changing oneself in one's family relationships needs rehearsal. This repetitious mental rehearsal will give better odds for success in the actual emotional arena of the family intensities.

Doing it Differently

One can make contact, observe, think, plan, and rehearse forever. But if there are no real behavioral changes in the actual relationships, basic level of self will remain the same. So finally, we have to enter the family arena and "do ourselves differently" in those relationships.

We shrink most from this difficult part of the work because we sense that the family will react if we change our functional position that is so familiar to all. We fear this reaction. Perhaps the most difficult and somewhat predictable part of differentiation of self in one's family is managing oneself around the family system's reaction to the change in self.

It is true that when one does not play the accustomed role in the emotional pattern, and instead becomes more of a self in the system, or when one takes a step out of the family emotional process, the system will react with various intense expressions of emotions. It is the "change back" message and it may take the form of threats or criticism. Intensity may increase in the family triangles. *However, if one works at staying in calm contact with family members involved, not reacting back, not trying to change others, simply managing one's own reactivity, those reactions will subside.* Soon after that, the differentiating person can become aware of a higher level of individual functioning.

Of course, the family relationships of people working in this way nearly always improve. One may actually be accorded a different position in the family. We often see various other family members showing evidence of better functioning as well. Often, the family seems to be "closer," with the relationships running more smoothly. As these steps are repeated over time, in different situations, with different family members, people consistently report a better level of functioning in all areas. These great results stem from better relationship functioning in their own families.

Changing the patterned ways of reacting and moving within one's family is so basic that when any progress is made, the basic self emerges fundamentally changed. Likely the nervous system makes structural and even biochemical changes. More neutrality and less reactivity will have been attained when one can enter into meaningful discussions with people without criticizing, defending, or attacking. Many confrontations and showdowns can be avoided in this way. Relationships work better.

The project will be more effective if one can learn about the individuals who peopled the generations of one's family. It is surprising how much can be learned about relatives who are long gone. A family diagram is a huge assist in this effort. Such a diagram not only places each individual in a nuclear family but also charts important facts such as locations, educational attainment, health status, and occupations. Dates of births, moves, deaths, and immigration are all recorded on the diagram. Thus, it becomes a necessary document, summarizing a great deal of information (See figure 15.1). After this information is recorded, relationship patterns of functioning, facts regarding family members, and relationship patterns in nuclear units can be ascertained, often from older members of the family.

Stories told by older generations as well as by family friends may reveal trends, such as themes passed down through the family. Some examples of themes are achievement, conflict, distance, violence, cutoff, or survival. Relationship patterns among family members may eventually be seen through this kind of detective work. All this adds life and breath to the bones of the simple genealogy of the family diagram.

If the goal is to know self and work with one's own patterns, the highest yield comes from going back to the extended family alone, without others present. If the reactivity with mother and father is too great, it is possible to postpone working on differentiation there for awhile, going instead to the families from which they came, learning what one can about their parents and siblings as well as other family members. This effort can be extremely productive. If these people are dead, it is sometimes possible to find people who were emotionally important to parents. Friends of parents might have been an important part of their emotional field, providing another opening on better understanding.

At times people are in a cut off position that blocks them from this kind of effort, even though, intellectually, they might see its potential benefits. Old grudges, hurts, or feeling patterns impede their efforts. A knowledge of family systems theory helps people get past this. The current cutoff is probably only this generation's version of a family response to intensity that may be seen in several generations. As one pushes past the cutoff tendency, there will be a fundamental change in the self and the cutoff tendency will be predictably less strong in the next generation.

As one makes contact with family, understands them more, and functions more maturely in one's family system, while thinking systems—seeing as much of the total complex picture as possible— cause-and-effect thinking, blame, and criticism drop off. Learning to know as many people in one's extended family as possible will often lead to a growing acceptance of all members of the family. This acceptance, which grows out of a view from a wider lens, is neither critical nor competitive.

It is important to be clear that working on differentiating a self out of one's family of origin is not:

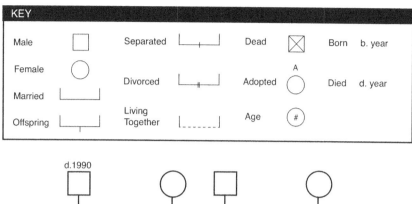

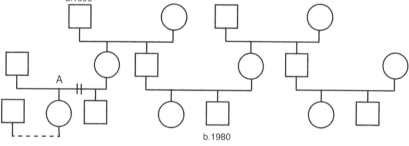

Figure 15.1. A family diagram. Family diagrams are records of the facts of family history. Birth dates, death dates, locations, moves with dates, education, and health are all recorded on it.

- Doing therapy on the family,
- Getting people to express feelings,
- Talking over issues,
- Rehashing past slights, grudges, or deficiencies,
- Blaming anyone for the way things have turned out, or
- "Sharing," or "dumping" one's feelings.

Rather, with focus mostly on managing self (not the others) differentiating requires moving to a different level of comfort and responsibility in one's family. It may not involve much talk at all in some families. In others it may. In its simplest terms, *efforts at differentiation amount to becoming a better version of oneself in one's own family relationships.*

Different tactics must be employed in peaceful, agreeable families from those in explosive families. In a peaceful family, one sometimes must get emotions stirred up in order to see the triangles and emotional process. If this strategy is used in a more emotionally intense family, however, one courts disaster. In all our families, there are some difficult relationships that we naturally avoid. But if we will *go toward them instead* we will learn the most about relationships. *It is not in the easy relationships that we make the longest strides in managing self.*

Work on the self in one's family of origin becomes, for those who take it on, a profound adventure that carries with it a life-changing effect. Clinical evidence is mounting that changing one's relationships with the people one grew up with exerts a much more powerful effect on self than simply talking about those relationships with a therapist. But a coach who has been there in his or her own family will be a useful and necessary guide through the effort. Many who have taken up this challenge report it to be a rewarding and worthwhile endeavor, not only in developing individual strengths but also in functioning better in all relationships.

Thinking It Over

Of all the strategies toward better relationships, the most important one yet devised may be working to be more present, accountable, and responsible in the family, out of understanding and acceptance. That amounts to working more out of basic self in all of one's family relationships.

Real Life Research

1. How clear are you on your guiding principles?

2. On which would you like to do further thinking or research?

3. Of all the steps of working in one's family on self, which ones do you predict will be the most difficult for you?

4. On your family diagram, where do you see cutoff?

5. Which relationships on your family diagram will be the most challenging for you to begin and/or continue?

6. Can you think of ways to find information about relatives who have died?

7. Are there elders in your family who may be resources to you in your efforts?

8. How hard is it for you to go to your family without trying to change it?

9. Who are you "allergic" to in your family?

10. With whom will you welcome having more contact?

11. Are there ways you could step up to becoming a more responsible family member?

Endnotes

1. Bowen, Murray, *Family Therapy in Clinical Practice,* Jason Aronson, New York, 1978, p. 316.

2. *Ibid.,* p. 371.

3. *Ibid.,* p. 540.

4. *Ibid.,* p. 317.

5. *Ibid.,* p. 216.

MANAGING THE INTENSITIES

The instinctual force for differentiation is built into the organism, just as are the emotional forces that oppose it.[1] (1976)

It is reasonably accurate to compare the functioning of the emotional and intellectual systems to the structure and function of the brain.[2] (1976)

The human phenomenon is serious and tragic, but at the very same time, there is a comical or humorous aspect to most serious situations.[3] (1971)

Murray Bowen

If we can change only self, and if it is emotional intensity that tends to sidetrack relationships, how do we think about managing the emotional intensities in self as they arise? What does it mean to manage oneself better emotionally in relationships?

Until now it has been emphasized that issues of managing self in relationships can be brought into therapy and solved there. Originally, by those working in the "old theory," it was hoped that the effort to work out feelings toward and with the therapist would then modify patterns in all relationships. This was useful to some degree.

In Bowen theory, if strong repetitive or other types of interfering patterns arise, they are usually seen to be life-long. And they are best dealt with in the original family system where they first developed. But, if issues arise in any relationship, they can be taken up in the relationship. Partners can best work toward neutrality in the context of the relationship situation rather than in the coaching situation.

Taking Feelings into Relationships

The therapy profession has typically had one answer to the question, "How do I handle my feelings?" The answer has been, "Talk it out." Certainly it works that way in the consulting room. If one can talk it out with a professional listener, one usually will leave the room feeling better. But there, one of the two is being paid to stay calm. Furthermore, does this experience of getting to calm in the therapist's office lead to any long-term resolution or step-up in life functioning? Often it does not seem to.

In any case, attempting to manage feelings in other relationships—where no one is being paid to stay calm—by talking out all feelings, often burdens relationships with more emotional intensity than they can bear. Certainly, there may be times when it is appropriate to process feelings in a relationship. However, if relationships are the court of first resort for processing feelings, the relationships most often will run into trouble. The relationship is kept in such a state of excitement that it begins to be a burden to each.

Processing an Emotional/Feeling State

Most often, feelings are best processed by each individual alone, each taking responsibility only for his or her own feelings. How exactly does one process a feeling reaction? A few steps are suggested:

1. Observe it. Step away mentally to see and feel what is actually going on inside. Where in the body is the hurt or tension? Where is the anxiety being carried? What is the feeling?

2. Calm it. Calm the feeling as soon as possible. "As soon as possible," may take a while, but as soon as the feeling is located physically, let it go physically. Don't prolong any emotional intensity. Taking a few slow, deep breaths, relaxing muscles or physical exercise may help to calm a feeling state. Remember, too, that *cerebral activity inhibits emotional centers of the brain.* So, if one can begin cerebral activity (that is not fired by the lower centers) such as *reading* or *logical thinking*, it may be easier to get to calm.

3. Think about it. In the thoughtful processing of feelings, certain questions are useful. The include:

- **What triggered the reactivity?** In order to determine this, it is useful to place the onset of the anxiety in time: When did it begin? Just before that, what was going on? Using this rather meticulous approach, one can often identify the trigger.

- **Is this trigger-feeling response a pattern?** Is it one that I experience on a regular basis? If so, what is this feeling pattern about? Rejection? Competition? Someone from the past who reacted this way in my family? Is it a repetition reaction?

- **Is this an appropriate response at this time, given this particular trigger?** Why now? Is there another anxiety trigger I am missing here?

- **If this is not a desired response, are there other response options I would like in my repertoire?** What could they be? Don't forget about humor. It can dispel anxiety fast if it is not overused so as to avoid dealing with the realities of a situation.

4. Choose the best response option and rehearse it. Imagine what it would be/feel like to respond that way.

5. Make the new response a pattern. Practicing in real life a well as in one's head frequently helps the response become more automatic. Eventually, these repetitions in relationships—at work, in friendships, in the nuclear family, and of course, in one's family of origin—will replace an old feeling pattern with a new, more appropriate and useful one.

One of the main goals in managing oneself in relationships is to be able to be less reactive to the feeling states of those around one. At the same time, communications are kept open in order to remain accessible to others. The self-boundary stays intact.

To summarize the steps in processing feelings and changing patterns of reactivity, the following three words come up again:

- **Observe** the emotional state within the self and the system as well as the trigger.
- **Think** about what has been observed and how to make sense of it through "the lens" of systems thinking. Plan a different way of responding next time and rehearse it.
- **Act.** No reactive pattern ever changed simply by understanding it. There will be plenty of chances—systems tend to repeat their patterns.

If one doesn't hash out all the feeling states with the other, isn't this simply "stuffing them down," as we have been taught by the (old) therapy profession? Won't they cause trouble later as Freud thought? He believed the feelings went into the unconscious mind, only to erupt later in some form or other.

In systems thinking, there is no unconscious. Feeling states are simply that. *They come and they go.* For the most part calming them and beginning to think about options as soon as possible does far less damage than expressing, explaining, or dragging the other into them. There are some times when we might want to go over feelings with our partner. These are much rarer than we might think, because it only takes one to process anxiety within and to work on changing emotionally patterned functioning. These efforts will change the relationship for the better. When we do decide to process feelings in the relationship, it is wise to wait until the intensity has passed so that people can talk more reasonably about them as well as options for going forward.

Dealing with Crisis

It is impossible for there to be more than relative separation between emotional and intellectual functioning, but those whose intellectual functioning can retain relative autonomy in periods of stress are more flexible, more adaptable and more independent of the emotionality about them. They cope better with life stresses, their life courses are more orderly and successful and they are remarkably free of human problems.[4]

Every relationship goes through periods of special stress. This occurs most notably when someone enters or leaves the relationship system of which the primary relationship is a part. Examples of this type of stress are marriage, births of children, deaths in the family, or divorce. These are referred to as "nodal events." At these times, anxiety in the system goes up. Other types of stress, however, can certainly affect relationships intensely enough to precipitate a crisis.

A crisis can be defined as *a period of rapid change, in which individual functioning is sometimes permanently altered, either toward a higher or lower level.* Clinical evidence indicates that relationships also can change to higher or lower levels of functioning for very long periods of times after an important event.

Nodal Events

Bowen wrote about events that disturb family functioning:

The equilibrium of the unit is disturbed by either the addition of a new member or the loss of a member. The intensity of the emotional reaction is governed by the functioning level of integration in the family at the time or by the functional importance of the one who is added to the family or lost to the family. For instance, the birth of a child can disturb the emotional balance until family members can realign themselves around the child. A grandparent who comes for a visit may shift family emotional forces briefly, but a grandparent who comes to live in a home can change the family emotional balance for a long period. Losses that can disturb the family equilibrium are physical losses, such as a child who goes away to college or an adult child who marries and leaves the home. There are functional losses, such as a key family member who becomes incapacitated with a long-term illness or injury that prevents his doing the work on which the family depends. There are emotional losses, such as the absence of a light-hearted person who can lighten the mood in a family. A group that changes from light-hearted laughter to seriousness becomes a different kind of organism. The length of time required for the family to establish a new emotional equilibrium depends on the emotional integration in the family and the intensity of the disturbance . . . An attempt to get the family to express feelings at the moment of change does not necessarily increase the level of emotional integration.[5]

The Shock Wave

The "emotional shock wave" phenomenon was described by Bowen as a reaction to an event by the system that can have effects on it over an extended time.

It occurs most often after the death of a significant family member, but it can be almost as severe after a threatened death. . . . A grandmother in her early sixties . . . had a radical mastectomy for cancer. Within the following two years, there was a chain of serious reactions in her children and their families. One son began drinking for the first time in his life, the wife of another son had a serious depression, a daughter's husband failed in business and another daughter's children became involved in automobile accidents and delinquency. Some symptoms were continuing five years later when the grandmother's cancer was pronounced cured.[6]

When anxiety intensifies in an emotional system, it affects the thinking and behavior of the individuals of it. As their anxiety level increases, they become less adaptable. Relationship patterns, if present, will tend to become more intense and automatic. Thinking is more difficult at times of increased anxiety, so people may do or say things they cannot stand by in the long term. A greater effort than usual will be needed to manage one's emotions individually and in relationships.

During periods of unusual stress, or at any time of increased anxiety, standard "stress reduction" techniques, such as greater than usual amounts of physical and mental relaxation, are useful. Physically relaxed muscles moderate anxiety and promote clear-headedness. Anxiety may be greatly reduced by physical exercise and playful activities whether done alone or with others. At a time of crisis, there never seem to be enough hours in the day, so these activities may need to be intentionally planned.

Humor

A sense of humor can be incredibly useful when anxiety is high. It can, if not overused:

- Dispel the useless anxiety of a group,
- Help restore the big picture,
- Restore a sense of cooperation when needed, and
- Bring those good feelings so often associated with healing.

Relaxation and recreation, important as they are, must be balanced with finding ways of staying appropriately active in the crisis. Remaining in calm contact with as many people in a system as possible as the crisis unfolds is an active process. Quiet observation, the first step in understanding an anxious system, will of itself have a calming effect. It is the first of the steps that make thoughtful resolution possible in the end.

Nothing will ever be resolved, however, unless one is actively meeting the challenge. Thinking is essential, but so is action based on the thinking. Action based only on emotion, on the other hand, usually turns out to be worse than no action at all.

During times of crisis, the constant, conscious effort to process one's own feelings will result in big payoffs in relationships. This means putting a stop to needless, thoughtless dumping of feelings into the system in favor of habitually taking responsibility for the processing of one's own feelings and reactions. This does not mean that other people cannot be tremendous resources during a crisis or that some processing of feelings cannot be beneficial in relationships. Rather, it is a plea for a more judicious use of relationships for this purpose. After all, no one can deal with another's feelings for them. Processing feelings, in the final analysis, must be done by the self. Taking responsibility for one's feelings means learning greater and greater facility at processing those feelings. Out of this process comes the calm necessary to think one's way through a crisis.

Grief

Observing the grief process of people trained in Bowen theory has shows some striking contrasts to the popular understanding of the grief process. While theory-trained people miss their parent or spouse and have sad feelings, they seem to do better than people not trained in Bowen theory. *The difference observed was that they stayed in touch with the dead person's family of origin.* By doing that, they kept contact with the emotional system of which the dead person was only a part. Even though someone dies, the emotional process of the family still continues on. *The wider system—the original unit with its emotional process—is still available for contact.* By making contact with that system, it is possible that the people avoided cutoff, with its attendant intensity and symptoms. They functioned better than many people do at a time of loss. Is what is usually described in the stages and intensity of grief actually cutoff?

So, to reiterate, in a period of rapid change, individual and relationship functioning in an individual or a relationship system is changed toward a higher or a lower level, permanently, in some cases. How one handles one's emotions during a crisis—whether one is able to observe emotional process in the system, use that information, and think about various options—can have a profound effect on decision making, relationships and whether the event can be used to push the self up to a higher level of functioning.

Training in Self-Regulation

> The term *reflex* is accurate in that it occurs automatically and out of awareness, but like a reflex emotions can be brought within limited observation and under limited conscious control, just as one can control a knee jerk with specific energy.[7]

One important aid to improving emotional self-management, while working on differentiation of self in one's original family, can be self-regulation training, often referred to as biofeedback training.

Dr. Elmer Green, one of the pioneers in the development of biofeedback training, said in 1969:

> Every change in the physiological state is accompanied by an appropriate change in the mental-emotional state . . . and conversely, every change in the mental-emotional state . . . is accompanied by an appropriate change in the physiological state."[8]

Self knowledge is the *sine qua non* out of which high-level relationship skills develop. So if one can pay close enough attention to the self and one's reactivity at every level possible, one will be able to develop a degree of mastery of a factual base that applies to all one's relationship systems.

In 1910, combining concepts derived from hypnosis, medical research, and logic, German psychiatrist Johannes Schultz developed a system of self-regulation he called "autogenic training," that is, self-generated or self-willed training. He recommended six exercises. They were designed to induce heaviness, peripheral warmth, heart rate regulation, respiratory control, abdominal warmth and cooling of the forehead. With these exercises, he obtained a measure of control over changes in attention, consciousness, thought, and emotion.

Through the years, the study of regulating automatic functions of the body has continued. Today's technology makes it possible to attach leads to various parts of the body and detect and amplify signals of minute changes we are not ordinarily aware of. The signals can be routed to a computer monitor, bringing them to visual awareness. They can also be transformed into sounds heard in earphones, bringing them to auditory awareness. The "feedback" gives us awareness of processes we usually know nothing about. *All it takes to be able to control a bodily process is to bring it to consciousness.*[9] In this way, many processes that are normally out of awareness become available for modification.

On the cutting edge of behavioral science, the development of biofeedback training represents a major advance in the understanding of physiological/emotional processes. The relationships between stress, relationships and physiology become clearer when the reactivity can actually be seen or heard.

Muscular relaxation is incompatible with anxiety.[10] Since muscular tension level is usually outside of awareness, there was no way to access it to lower anxiety. But, with the advent of biofeedback, people could learn to recognize their levels of muscular tension and could learn to intentionally interrupt their anxiety and relax. This ability to relax muscular tension can be invaluable in the midst of relationship intensity. It can actually calm the anxiety. Since calm is infectious in a relationship system (an emotional unit), if one person can achieve calm, the rest of the unit may often follow suit.

This ability to calm anxiety allows a person greater choice between automaticity and control. It is a way of breaking into one's emotional and physiological patterns, changing their direction, and giving greater flexibility in one's reactions. Since so much of relationship distress comes out of inadequately processed and managed anxiety, any tool that aids in the management of anxiety automatically enhance a relationship.

Presently, there are four major areas of biofeedback training. They are:

1. Reduction of muscle tension,
2. Galvanic skin response, the sweat response of skin (increases under anxiety),

3. Skin temperature training: the warmer the skin of extremities, the more relaxed the person is, and
4. Neurofeedback or electrical brain wave training (the newest development).

Less commonly, biofeedback training has also been used to lower blood pressure. It has also been found useful in many conditions such as asthma, addictions, migraine, diabetes, and various conditions of the reproductive system.[11] Neurofeedback, training of the electrical activity of the brain, is being found to be useful in all of these, as well as various brain conditions such as attention deficit disorder, hyperactivity, obsessive-compulsive disorder, and bipolar disorder.

Dr. Elmer Green describe it as follows:

> After a bad psychological habit is consciously replaced with a good habit, it need not remain in the forefront of consciousness. Everyone know this is true in the striate[12] domain, as when we learn to drive a car or play a musical instrument, but it is also true in the autonomic[13] domain. When a more relaxed, poised, alert, sensitive way of life becomes habitual, it no longer needs to be consciously practiced. It literally becomes a way of life. This is the goal of . . . training . . . whatever the problem . . . the number of successes makes the game worthwhile.[14]

Until recently it was believed that the autonomic (automatic) nervous system was not controllable voluntarily (except by certain yogis). Biofeedback technology, because it brings into consciousness processes normally unavailable to conscious monitoring, makes it possible for almost anyone to learn to control and modify automatic reactions.

Biofeedback training is a powerful tool for learning to choose between the emotional/feeling system and the intellectual system. At special times of stress for a relationship or for self, autogenic (biofeedback) training can make a great difference in one's ability to handle life crises well. Not only does the training make it possible to give self more comfort at will, but also because of the ability to calm anxiety, one can think more clearly under pressure, so that appropriate action can be taken.

Factual evidence for relationship systems such as the nuclear family operating as emotional units can be obtained in the biofeedback laboratory. There, whole families can be monitored simultaneously. Under those conditions, an emotional response can be seen to travel through the group. More and more, it becomes apparent how the automatic responses of individuals in relationship postures such as triangles are inextricably linked.[15]

The ability to remain relaxed at will means one can stay calm and thoughtful when one's partner is anxious. If one can remain calm in the presence of another's anxiety, many a situation will be saved from escalating to a crisis point.

Further, the ability to choose emotions, to manage physiology, and to control anxiety as one challenges one's patterns of reactivity, all help in defining self-boundaries.

Addictions

Fifteen people struggled with addictions to prescription tranquilizers and sleeping medications. In consultation, their addicted behavior was understood in the context of relationship postures and anxiety. *They were, without exception, in an underfunctioning position in their significant relationships.* The relationship anxiety, however, was magnified greatly by the intense anxiety that was a symptom of withdrawal from the medications. Of the fifteen, three took advantage of biofeedback relaxation training to help with the withdrawal.

The three stood out from the group in several ways. They made many fewer panicky calls to the therapist. They experienced the same anxiety of withdrawal as the rest of the group but, using the new responses they had learned in their training, were able to calm the anxiety they experienced without resorting to hospitalization or medication. Best of all, they reported that—as they gained control of their feeling states through the use of biofeedback training as well as using knowledge of the relationship principles they learned in the consultation—they were able to function more as equals in their relationships. In this way, they worked directly on the root of the problem that initially led to addiction, that is, their underfunctioning posture in relationships.[16]

How does relaxation training improve relationship functioning? These addicted people described how, when relationship patterns threatened to snap into place, carrying their attendant anxiety, the voluntary muscular system tensed up and further fed their anxiety. The relaxation response, by interfering with anxiety, made it possible for them to keep thinking. The ability to think in an anxious relationship field made it possible to be more of a self in their relationships. That went hand in hand with getting out of the under functioning position.

Mr. M explains:

> When my boss comes at me tense and demanding I'm able more of the time now to go into my relaxation mode. Maybe not at the exact moment he is coming at me, but very soon afterwards I'm able to. I can think about what an appropriate response from me would be. I can approach him with a calm manner and an answer that is thought out. He becomes reasonable, which surprises me—I mean, the way one person being calm can affect the mood of the other person. The same thing has been true with my relationship with my girlfriend. When she begins to plan my life, I can now back off mentally, relax a little and instead of just going into shutdown, keep thinking. I can decide what it is I think and what I want to do or not do and then give her my input. She actually seems to appreciate my being more active in the relationship. She is getting the idea now, too. When I slip back into my old pattern and ask her for advice that I don't really need, she usually makes a joke that lets me know she is thinking about relationship patterns, trying to stay out of them!

As the anxiety level of the relationship dropped, the relationship inequality diminished, and the symptom (the addiction) simply was not there.

Biofeedback training shows us worlds more than we have known before about the interplay between emotions, physiology, and relationships. In addition to providing that knowledge, it is becoming a powerful new tool in modifying that interplay. Neurofeedback, the newest and most powerful form of biofeedback, can actually teach us to change maladaptive brainwave patterns. Research is accumulating to support its effectiveness in treating a variety of symptoms. It may eventually replace older forms of biofeedback training.

Thinking It Over

Emotional intensity can make logical problem-solving, thinking, or appropriate relationship responses impossible. Since anxiety is central to relationship difficulties, learning to regulating one's automatic responses is key to better relationship functioning. It can help get to a calmer thinking position, one that is useful in a relationship. Also, getting to logical thinking can modify unwanted emotional responses.

Real Life Research

1. Can you think of times when you have been able to interrupt your automatic relationship responses? How did you do it?

2. How good are you at relaxing?

3. How good at interrupting anxiety?

4. Who is the calmest person you have ever known?

5. Do you have a symptom that might yield to being more of a self in a relationship (while not overfunctioning)?

6. How do other people try to get you to take on their anxiety? How good are you at staying out?

7. In family times of loss or crisis, who have you observed to be the most reactive? Who is the calmest?

8. How automatic is it for you to reach for food, a pill, or some other substance to calm anxiety? Would there be another way to do it?

9. How useful is your sense of humor to you in anxious times?

10. What are some new ways of handling anxiety you would like to develop?

Endnotes

1. Bowen, Murray, *Family Therapy in Clinical Practice,* Jason Aronson, New York, 1978, p. 371.

2. *Ibid.*, p. 372.

3. *Ibid.*, p. 250.

4. *Ibid.*, p. 362.

5. *Ibid.*, p. 325.

6. *Ibid.*, p. 326.

7. *Ibid.*, p. 422.

8. Green, Elmer. Training conference or professionals the author attended in 1969.

9. Green, Elmer, in lectures given at the Menninger Clinic in the 1970's.

10. Ibid.

11. Harrison, Victoria, "Reproduction and Emotional Cutoff," in *Emotional Cutoff*, Peter Titelman, ed., Haworth, New York, 2003, p. 245.

12. The striate muscles are the ones that are normally under conscious control, as opposed to the smooth muscles of the gastrointestinal system that operate automatically, out of awareness. They are called striate (or smooth) because of their striped appearance (or not) under the microscope. The system of striate muscles is considered to be fairly easily trainable, as for example in athletics. The autonomic or involuntary nervous system, on the other hand, ordinarily has nothing to do with voluntary control. It makes automatic

adjustments of organs such as the heart, blood vessels and bronchial tubes. They all have "smooth" muscles.

13. The autonomic nervous system operates automatically, out of awareness.

14. Green, Elmer, "Some Historical Notes on the Biofeedback Research Society: Leading to its Formation in October 1969" in *Biofeedback*, Winter, 1989.

15. In many presentations, Priscilla Friesen, Victoria Harrison, and others have described in detail the reactivity of one family member to another, as seen on biofeedback equipment.

16. Gilbert, Roberta, "Addiction to Prescribed Medication," *Family Systems*, 1994, No.1:1.

TEN RELATIONSHIP MISCONCEPTIONS AND TEN NEW WAYS OF THINKING

I did not agree with the numerous misinterpretations of theory about the human family, but I am also never in favor of telling others what they should believe.[1]

Murray Bowen, 1988

Most people bring a few misconceptions into their relationships. Here are some common ones.

1. "My partner will make me happy." Happiness (and the pursuit of it) is an individual matter. It could be said to be a choice at higher levels of functioning. Using others as a mood trigger is a boundary violation. Another person may enhance or detract from one's happiness, but at high levels of functioning the primary responsibility for happiness or lack of it remains with the self.

2. "I can change the other," or "If you cared about me you would . . . ". Serious boundary intrusions such as this set both people up for disappointment. Most relationships cannot bear that kind of load. The sooner this belief and effort is given up, the better the relationship will fare. As with happiness, change is accomplished only by and for each individual.

3. "If I work on differentiation of self I'll become cold and unfeeling." What the work actually does is to give one more choice in the use of thinking and feeling systems as well as to free more self from relationship fusions. At high levels of functioning the thinking and feeling systems are integrated and working well together. At that level, the emotional system is more able to be employed in the service of the intellectual rather than the other way around. Life becomes freer of problems—the kind most of us bring on ourselves. People important to each other say they are closer than they ever have been.

4. "It is my right to respond from my emotions to my partner's anxiety." The excuse usually given for this misconception is, "It is too hard not to," followed by, "Why should I do all the work?" When one responds to anxiety with anxiety it leads to escalation, intensification, and an unstable relationship. Trying instead to see the other's anxiety states and whatever he or she does or says during them as the other persons emotional "trash" may be more useful. Most useful is to do what one does with trash—throw it out!²

5. "This relationship will never get any better." If one truly believes that, it probably won't. But how can one tell? Since any relationship can function at a better level if even one person in it changes, either has the power to start to change things for better functioning at any time. It is really the only viable option.

6. "I've changed myself all I can and things aren't any better." To be alive is to change, so this limitation has to be a misconception even as it is being spoken. Nevertheless, two people never change at the same time. If one partner has actually raised their level of differentiation, that one will have more patience. Giving the relationship time to adjust to the changes in level of maturity and giving a partner time to come up to a new level of functioning, can make a huge difference.

7. "Whenever I need to talk it out or get my feelings out, my partner must agree to listen." The beliefs that talking about feelings is the only way to feel better or that relationships exist for the purpose of processing feelings is commonly accepted by today's culture. Communicating is a high priority for any well-functioning relationship. But at a particular moment the other may or may not be ready for the task.

There are many ways to change feeling states. The nature of feelings is that they come and go. Talking them out is only one of many ways to affect these states. It is probably a way that, if used exclusively, no relationship can tolerate. If one can take primary responsibility for processing one's feelings and be selective about which feeling-based issues to bring into the relationship, it will do better.

8. "I continue to worry about the past." One's own or the other person's obsessions can defeat relationships. The belief that blaming one's partner or members of one's family of origin somehow help one advance is especially prevalent in our society. However, if the past can be relegated to the past, most relationships will benefit from this choice and flourish.

9. "If you don't love me like my mother did, you don't love me at all."[3] Only one person will ever love one like one's mother.

10. "I can cut off from my extended family and still have good relationships. In fact, they will probably be better." A family of origin cutoff stacks the odds heavily against good nuclear family or other present relationships. For one thing, the anxiety has fewer places to go, so relationships by definition are more intense.

Ten New Ways of Thinking About Human Interactions

> The "I position" defines principle and action in terms of, "This is what I think or believe" and "This is what I will do or will not do," without impinging one's own values or beliefs on others.[4]

> **Murray Bowen, 1972**

Here are some statements one might hear from people successfully thinking Bowen family systems theory in their primary relationships.

1. "When I work toward my own emotional calm and intellectual objectivity, I think more clearly. My messages, actions, and emotional contribution to the relationship are positive assets to it rather than liabilities. For example, I stay on the subject." It is not necessary to be a victim of the emotional climate of others. Taking responsibility for one's full fifty percent in the relationship makes a huge difference.

2. "I am at my best in relationships when I can observe myself in a relationship pattern and change my part in it without any expectations of the other." Managing the emotional (undifferentiated, automatic) self is a huge task for most of us. It is probably the biggest part of the work that must be done in relationships.

3. "Staying in contact and maintaining one-to-one relationships with the individuals in my systems is important for me. It provides a sense of groundedness I have in no other way." People caught in the cutoff pattern of their family generations tend to perpetuate it into the next generation. Invariably they find that this works no better for them than it did for previous generations. A cutoff system is an intense system. Intensity translates into relationship difficulties.

4. "It doesn't matter who initiates the contact or if one person makes more than his or her share of contacts. What matters is that they are made." To be present and accounted for, especially in a relatively cut off system, may mean that one sometimes gets the feeling that one is doing more than one's share of the work. However, people who function at higher levels, while they are calmer, are also active forces in the system. So, if one is doing more than others in the system, it can be seen as a marker of a better level of functioning.

5. "If I can remember to look for the anxiety behind the attempted boundary intrusions of others, I can be less reactive,

managing myself better around them. After all, they are automatic and not intentional." Anxious communications call for better-than-usual attempts to manage the emotional self. If the other person is seen as simply anxious (rather than as pompous, overbearing, arrogant, or malicious) he or she can be dealt with differently.

6. "It is not necessary for me to take on the emotions of the people I am around. I have choices." As one pushes up to higher levels of differentiation, not only is there more choice between thinking and automatic reactions, but self boundaries are also more intact. The emotional reactions of others can thus remain theirs.

7. "I do not need to be loved, liked, approved of, accepted or nurtured by people around me." At lower levels of differentiation, approval of others can be an orienting factor, but as one moves up in functioning, it is less needed. It becomes more important to be clear about one's own inner guidance. Approval and acceptance are taken into consideration but they are not the primary motivators.

8. "Keeping my focus primarily on efforts to manage myself (at least fifty-one percent of the time), remembering to use guiding principles, and keeping in touch with my family of origin, I can usually find ways to do better without being overly critical of myself or blaming anyone else. Focusing that amazing brain on the functioning of the self, especially the emotional self, is itself a high-level function. We can all get better at it with practice.

9. "Important relationship decisions, if made calmly and thoughtfully, stand the test of time better than those that I impulsively rush into guided primarily by feelings." Clinical evidence corroborates daily that those who run their lives mostly in the world of feelings, making their decisions by how they feel, rather than by a careful, objective thought process, live in a world of chaotic relationships.

10. "I work toward needing less togetherness. But, acting on principle, I can choose companionship and cooperative group effort when that is the best use of my life energy." *At high levels of differentiation people can be happy in or out of relationships.* They are complete and do not need others to complete them. Perhaps partly because of the lack of pressing need for them, their relationships function better. They have more energy to do what makes the best use of their talents and abilities as they make their unique contributions in the world.

Thinking It Over

Many of our guiding principles about relationships come from "old theory," our family of origin, or from the culture at large. These may or may not be useful. Using the new lens, a set of principles emerges that describes the relationship world more accurately.

Real Life Research

1. How many relationship principles can you think of that are not serving you well?

2. In each case, what was the origin of the principle? Family? School?

3. From your family, using the lens of the new theory, what principles do you think you want to keep?

4. How often do you make the connection between the need for family connectedness and your relationship success?

5. What unrealistic expectations tend to weight down your relationships?

Endnotes

1. Bowen, Murray, in Kerr, Michael E. and Murray Bowen, *Family Evaluation,* W. W. Norton, New York, 1988, p. 384.
2. After comments made by Kathleen Kerr during coaching sessions at the Georgetown Family Center.
3. Kerr, Michael E., in lectures given at the Bowen Center through the years.
4. Bowen, Murray, *Family Therapy in Clinical Practice,* Jason Aronson, New York, 1978, p. 495.

A GUIDEBOOK FOR ALL
RELATIONSHIPS

The goal . . . is to rise up out of the emotional togetherness that binds us all.[1]

Murray Bowen, 1976

Whenever the principles of family systems theory are applied and people begin to raise their functioning as individuals and in relationships, they are able to step up and do better in more than one area of their lives. From a higher level of emotional maturity, they discover they are more able to manage themselves in many situations. All their relationships begin to work better. With less relationship distress, there is more clarity and direction for going toward other goals. There is also more energy available for the best use of their talents.

When guided by relationship principles taken from systems thinking, maintaining meaningful relationships with one's own family of origin spawns an emotional "groundedness," or calm, of its own. This is true even when that family is involved in fairly turbulent emotional patterns. The degree to which one can step back from family emotions and still stay connected with individuals in the system will become an important determining factor for success in life. The facts one learns about the self in that family and the use one makes of these facts to further emotional maturity will influence all relationships for the better.

If the larger size of the human cerebrum is related to the larger and more complex social systems in which the human exists,[2] it follows that as one works on managing self better in relationships, that work will actually change brain physiology and anatomy.

To paraphrase Bowen: "That which is created in a relationship can be changed in a relationship."[3] Except for the fear of others' anxiety, there is no need to triangle, distance from, or cut off from one's relationships. Any of the work one does on oneself in one important relationship will pay off in all the others. Functioning better in one's family of origin not only helps functioning in that family but also in the nuclear family, the workplace, and in friendships. By the same token, if one undertakes to do a little better in workplace relationships, one soon finds that improved functioning there has also paid off in better family relationships. Because of fundamental changes in the brain and in thinking, life learning accomplished in one arena spills over into others.

The following are some of the many kinds of relationships where new ideas make a difference.

Friendships

> The theory states that the triangle, a three-person emotional configuration, is the molecule, or the basic building block of any emotional system, whether it is in the family or any other group. The triangle is the smallest stable relationship system.[4]

Friendship may be the ideal paradigm for all relationships. Many problems common to more intense relationships happen less frequently or not at all in friendships. If all relationships could be managed more like friendships, much difficulty in relationships could be avoided. Why is it that relationships between friends follow a smoother course than relationships between parents and children, employers and employees, and even lovers?

One explanation is that self is lost or gained less in friendships. In any relationship where that is the case, people can be more objective, reasonable, and useful to self and to each other. Because friendships are less in fusion, the intense automatic reactions come up less often.

In addition, a sense of play is preserved, affording relaxation and lowering the emotional intensity and subsequent anxiety present in the relationship. When anxiety is lower, each person can maintain equality, openness, and separate self boundaries more easily. In short, less self is fused into friendships. If one could think of children, spouses, or parents as our friends, what differences would there be in those relationships? What adjustments need to be made to move toward a paradigm of friendship in all relationships?

Friends are part of one's personal emotional system, a system other than family that broadens and deepens with the passage of years. In extraordinary relationships between friends, openness and availability do not migrate toward togetherness. Friends, at best, treat each other as equals. Although friendship systems are often referred to as "support" systems, the simple term "friendship system" may be more appropriate since the term "support" implies a borrowing or lending of self. By thinking of the self as needing support, one is placing oneself in an underfunctioning posture.

Friendships will last only when the friends are at the same level of differentiation. In time, since friendships become emotionally significant relationships (and to the degree that selves are lost into fusions), all of the concepts that apply to any important relationship also hold for friendships. Though usually less intense, it is possible for the same relationship patterns to occur, depending on the levels of differentiation of the partners, their family patterns, and their sibling positions. The same principles can be used to think about and to change patterns that occur in friendships.

Emotional maturity is attractive to others. So as one works on increasing basic level of self, one's number of friends often increases. On the other hand, as people move to a higher level of differentiation, some friendships may be lost where contact is infrequent if there is a disparity in maturity levels.

Dr. Walter Toman's research on sibling position (see Appendices IV and V), revealed knowledge about friendship preferences. But as one goes to higher levels of differentiation, sibling position is less a determinant. Friendships can be more easily sustained with people from any sibling position.

People who, for whatever reason (such as intractable cutoff or attrition), have no family members available with whom to work on relationships can still make significant gains working on differentiation of self through a friendship system. They will, however, be much more successful if they can find some family relationships and work on improving their functioning there.

Working to see family relationships more as friendships can have a great effect. Bowen's own words about making one's parents into one's best friends worked wonders in the life of the author. It is a paradigm that one can easily understand.

Love Relationships

> In broad terms, a person-to-person relationship is one in which two people can relate personally to each other about each other, without talking about others (triangling) and without talking about impersonal things. . . . In its ultimate sense, no one can ever know what a person-to-person relationship is, since the quality of any relationship can always be improved. On a more practical level, a person-to-person relationship is between two fairly well-differentiated people who can communicate directly, with mature respect for each other, without the complications between people who are less mature. The effort to work toward person-to-person relationships improves the relationship system in the family, and it is a valuable exercise in knowing self.[5]

How is it possible to nearly complete a book about relationships and rarely see the word "love"? Love is an interesting word. People think they know what they mean by it. But the problem comes in defining love and understanding what is being conveyed. It is one of the most ambiguous words in our language because of its emotional loading with specific personal life experience and emotional patterns. In the consulting room, people express their frustration with trying to understand what to expect from and how to behave in the state of love.

Another problem with the word "love" is how emotionally charged it is. To the extent that emotionally charged language is used in a thoughtful effort, the thinking runs the risk of becoming based more on emotion than thought. If based in emotion it would be less dependable, valid, or objective.

Love is used as a reason to stay together, and lack of love, a reason to terminate a relationship. This line of thinking is indulged in most often by people who are living their lives based more on emotions than on thinking or guidance by principle. Actually, research shows that when couples stay together through a period where they have lost positive feelings, within five years the feelings most often come back and the relationship endures over the long term.[6]

Bowen theory, with its goal of bringing the study of human behavior into the realm of science, puts a priority on objective, observable facts. Love, a subjective concept, is difficult, if not impossible, to bring into that realm. *The word "love," therefore, which generates more heat than light, was left out of the theory for some very good reasons.*

Mating and reproduction, necessary to survival of the species, are rooted in the automatic or emotional parts of the human. It is the feeling side of the mating process that is rhapsodized, sonnetized, and lyricized. Love feels so good. And most permanent relationships go through that phase. But often an intense "loving" relationship can bring on a veritable jungle of precarious feeling states. At these times, a thoughtful, substantial guide through the jungle is a welcome addition to the lyrics and sonnets. Bowen theory has been such a guide for many.

For relationships to get out of the intense roller coaster of ups and downs so often experienced, thought as well as feelings will have to be a more prominent part of the picture than is usual. *If people who are intensely attracted to one another could stop short of engaging in sexual contact (which intensifies the feelings, making good decisions less likely) and revel in the delights of a separate, open, and equal friendship for a protracted period, it is probable that those relationships would have more chance for long-term success.* Under those conditions, people would have more chance to explore guiding principles in a thoughtful way. Then they could learn whether it is possible to think independently in the company of the other and see if a long term friendship, upon which all solid relationships must be based, is possible. It would be possible to see if the emotional system about to be developed would be to the mutual advantage of the two selves for further life development and high functioning.

Couples often see their problem as a sexual one. Sex therapists, however, find that by far the largest percentage of difficulties presented to them have much more to do with the way the relationship is working all the rest of the time than simply during sexual expression itself. That is, when relationships get on a more even keel, the couple's sexual problems disappear. Family therapists often make the same discovery. As people learn a new way of relating that makes it possible to think calmly together, with each managing his or her own emotions better over time, their relationship problems lessen and sexual attraction reappears on its own.

Does that mean high-level relationships are not intense and intensely loving? Not at all, but it may mean that the intensity, when it is there, will be more chosen and even to some degree controlled, rather than victimizing and dominating the relationship. Ideally, if the more emotionally neutral friendship stage of relationships could last much longer than it often does during the dating phase, couples could build a more substantial relationship base upon which to make a better decision about whether to intensify it. If, later, they decided to be intensely feeling and sexual with each other, sexual experience would be an expression of a solid relationship, one built over time. What we see all too often, however, is intense feelings generated too soon by people who may or may not be well matched for long term relationship success. Then, because of the attachment feelings generated by a sexual relationship,[7] they stay in a badly matched situation for longer than is useful for either.

At high levels of differentiation, a love relationship would ideally develop slowly and calmly, progressing from mutual attraction to an active, working, and long-lasting friendship. The friendship could sustain itself over the long term even as the intensities of feelings wax and wane. At high levels, with less emotional fusion to contend with, emotions would be chosen rather than dictating the situation. Spontaneity could still be present but there would simply be more choice more of the time. And, because boundaries are relatively separate, the relationship would not be subject to emotional piquing, escalation, and trading of self. Equality would not be an issue. It would simply be assumed and present in all actions and communications. Openness would be a given and the primary tool for problem-solving.

It has been said many times that the ability to love is based on one's ability to love oneself. What is the meaning of self love? People often have a problem thinking of how to love self. Yet they can readily fantasize loving another person. It may be that love of the self involves an ongoing relationship with the self, from a thinking point of view, that is all one would like relationships with others to be. That is, one works toward a realistic yet optimistic view of self, based on the facts, knowing where one still has work to do and always managing emotional reactivity. *This involves selecting some carefully considered guiding principles about how one thinks about oneself and making them a part of the guiding principle for basic self.*

What then is love? When all is said and done, what does it mean to love someone? The view of love derived from family systems theory may be different from any other. It is a refreshing view that stands in contrast to the view represented on television, in movies and in the culture in general. The most loving that one can be may at the same time be the most difficult way of being, requiring the best that is in oneself. A loving relationship requires effort to keep the big picture, emotional process, and one's principles constantly in mind. It requires effort to keep boundaries in mind, observed and intact. Equality and openness are present. If one loves, one will be loved, but not all the time.

Notwithstanding the comfort and excitement that togetherness can bring, perhaps the highest form of loving is simply to be able to maintain a separateness that focuses on being the best self one can be, while:

- Defining self to the other at appropriate times in a way that can be heard,
- Remaining in calm, thoughtful, meaningful contact with the other, and

- Accepting and making room for the efforts of the other at being the best he or she can be over time.

The Parent-Child Relationship

> The child-focused energy is deeply imbedded, and it includes the full range of emotional involvements from the most positive to the most negative. The higher the anxiety in the parents, the more intense the process.[8]

Being a parent may be the most difficult, anxiety-producing role in life. Perhaps this is because parents sense the importance of this role, adding to the pressure and thus increasing its level of difficulty. Fortunately, Bowen theory provides some guidelines. Because it is possible to push one's level of differentiation higher, it is possible, to some extent, to lessen the flow of undifferentiation into the next and future generations.

Like all relationships, the best parent-child relationships are characterized by separateness, openness, and equality. But how can a relationship between an adult and a child or infant be a relationship of equals? Of course, properly, it is not. However the parent who *looks toward* an eventual equal relationship with his or her offspring will be a different parent than the one who does not. That parent will have less of the automatic "overdoing for" posture that plays to the child's weaknesses. The relationship is a more cooperative one rather than being overfunctioning or competitive. Over time, the child will return this posture in kind.

Boundaries observed means that mutual respect between parent and child is fostered. Intact boundaries means less automatic reactivity. If the child is inordinately anxious, the parent can choose to stay calm. When anyone in a family is working on improving boundaries while respecting boundaries of others, the others in the family—sometimes rather quickly—do the same. Then it becomes less likely that anxiety and immaturity will come to rest in or get focused on any one member of the family. Just having the notion of boundaries clearly in mind makes it more likely that they are respected.

When guided by Bowen theory, open communication with the next generation differs from what is usually advocated and practiced. Notably, the oft-promoted preoccupation with feelings is absent. Although an understanding of others' feelings grows out of a well-developed understanding of one's own emotional systems (both internal and external to the self), it can be safely assumed that each individual is capable and adequate to the task of processing his or her own feelings. If one is respecting boundaries in interactions, it is not necessary to always check on the other's feelings—there will be fewer intrusions and thus less anxiety. Also, one is perfectly free, in such a system, to define feelings to the other, when that is important. So, although feelings are recognized, it is not necessary for parents and children to focus inordinately on them to the neglect of best thinking.

Openness in verbal communication with children implies a willingness to define one's principled thinking to them. Parents often seem to be afraid to say what they think to their children. It should not be taken for granted that offspring can infer what one is thinking. Often clinicians ask parents if they have ever told their children what they have just said to the clinician. Very often, parents answer, "They know what I think!" Actually, they may not. Theory guides us to define ourselves clearly and calmly to our youngsters in a way and at a time that they can hear. Of course, the opposite extreme, haranguing our kids about what we think is not useful either.

Speaking is done for self and only self. It is perfectly possible for a parent to clearly define his or her own principles to the next generation—principles carefully fashioned out of experience and thinking—without telling them what to do. That is, a parent can define self, while still respecting boundaries and the rights of people to differ and be different. Often, parents are reticent to talk about what they really believe in or to say what they really think.[9] But that is, after all, part of being a self in any relationship. And it is very useful to children to hear what principles guide their parents, even when they don't quite see it the way the parents do. With open communication, children will have the advantage of growing up around a self or two. Distance does not become a pattern.

As growing children and teenagers become more articulate, parents more often need to assume the role of an interested listener more of the time. Listening is a skill that many people in their parenting role, sadly, never learn. But how are children going to become able to define their thoughts and positions if no one ever listens to them, or values their ideas? As they mature, they are able to take on increased responsibility and can be included in more family decision-making. Only as they take responsibility for self do they get to the better levels on the scale.

Focusing on managing self and sustaining a well-functioning marriage precludes child-focus. And—although anxiety will travel around triangles as long as humans live in families—if open relationships are maintained, with each self making an effort to define self and no one else, there will be fewer casualties of the family emotional process. Conversely, if a child begins to draw a disproportionate amount of focus, it is safe to assume that anxiety generated in the spousal relationship has not been dealt with adequately. Instead of being resolved appropriately, it has become triangled into the child focus.

Unsurprisingly, when child-focus is lessened, the marital problem emerges. But it is far better to deal with it with the help of theory than to push the anxiety and the problem into the next generation. If anxieties are not resolved between the spouses, marital anxiety will continue to reverberate endlessly around the triangles of the family system. If a child becomes the center of an anxious parental focus, the child will carry a high degree of anxiety, immaturity, and eventually, symptoms—physical, mental/emotional, or social. Symptoms the child is at risk for can include underachievement at school, school phobias, depression, hyperactivity, psychosis, addictions, peer-relationship problems, rebelliousness, accident-proneness, vulnerability to physical illness, and many others.

If parents keep the focus on self-management in their own relationship, symptoms in the child will abate or disappear. Freed of the anxiety that was stifling personal progress, the child is able to get on with the process of developing a self. However, even when parents work very hard on their part of the problem, the symptoms of the focused child will sometimes reappear in the beginning of the effort. This is merely the system saying, "Change back." Child focus is a pattern that has been around awhile. Patterned behavior can take time to change. But if the parents stay on course with their own work, each time the symptoms reappear, they will be weaker and briefer. The problems of the child will eventually diminish significantly or disappear altogether.

Replacing the worried, anxious focus with confident interest in the child leaves the life problems of the child for the child to solve. The parents will stay alongside, interested, and in active communication, but they will not "take it on." It is an attitude that they have had all along toward other children in the family who are doing better. When parents take seriously the idea of differentiating a self in all the emotional systems of which they are a part, clarifying boundaries, and thinking and moving on principle, everyone in the emotional system benefits, especially growing children.

It is possible for a child-focused relationship to assume the form of any of the other relationship postures. The relationship can be distant, lack communication, or even be cut off at times. It can also be conflictual—openly fighting with each other or grappling with conformity or rebellion issues. Either parent or child can be in the over- or underfunctioning position.

But of all parental legacies, by far the best possible is that of raising one's own level of differentiation as high as possible in a lifetime. If that becomes the parental focus, the children will automatically function better.

Divorce

> The one who runs away . . . needs emotional closeness but is allergic to it . . . [and is] kidding himself that he is achieving "in-dependence." . . . The more intense the cutoffs with his parents

> the more he is vulnerable to repeating the same pattern in future relationships. . . . He can have an intense relationship in a marriage, which he sees as ideal and permanent at the time, but the physical distance pattern is part of him. When tension mounts in the marriage, he will use the same pattern of running away.[10]

Bowen theory does not advocate divorce. If the marital partners don't work on their own levels of differentiation of self to the extent that they can prevent divorce, they will simply find another partner with whom to replicate their immaturities. When families in the process of fracturing begin to work with principles of Bowen family systems theory, divorce often becomes unnecessary. And, unless one does move one's functioning to a higher level, divorce will probably solve nothing. The same immaturity and patterns of functioning will find ways of working themselves out in a succession of relationships that are no better than the former ones.

If divorce is a given, however, theory provides guidelines for managing it or moving through it. Keeping one's own anxiety processed will aid clear thinking, essential in any crisis. Being aware of the triangles and engaging them as they appear—in the family, partners, children, the legal profession, and the courts—is basic to managing the emotional self through such a time. Dilemmas can be addressed by anchoring oneself in facts, logic, and the bigger picture. Watching for emotional process can help to keep one more out of it, on course, and able to think.

After a divorce, it is often useful to reestablish emotionally neutral contact with the divorced partner as soon as possible if it has been lost during the legal process. If this can be done and continued over time, the mourning and devastating depression that can follow divorce is often less a factor. That depression may be intensified, however, by the effects of cutoff. Avoidance of cutoff is especially important if there are children. In contrast to those post-divorce relationships where chronic conflict, competition, or cutoff is the rule, if the two parents can preserve an emotionally calm working relationship, the children are the lifelong benefactors.

It is surprising to see what some families have accomplished in bridging divorce cutoffs. New spouses of remarriage can pose an initial challenge to the relating of two ex-spouses. But if the two persist because they realize how important to the welfare of their children their continued contact is, in time new spouses become more accepting.

Children in a divorced family can be expected to do about as well with the emotional process of divorce as the parents themselves do. But they can, as the family anxiety intensifies during such a time, absorb more than their share.[11] Even in a divorce, a child focus is not the optimal solution to problems that arise as a result of the emotional process.

Mrs. A remained cut off from her ex-husband three years after her divorce, except for necessary communications about their four-year-old daughter's visitation schedule. Mrs. A was depressed. Her daughter was manipulative and was noted by her teacher to have problems lying and hitting other children. Then Mrs. A, having learned some relationship principles by thinking systems with a coach, decided to try for a more open and cooperative relationship with her former husband. In the beginning of her effort he was suspicious of the change in her attitude, but she persisted. Rather than automatically reacting negatively when he asked for a change in visitation, she tried to accommodate whenever possible. If there was a problem with their daughter, rather than getting upset and keeping it to herself, she would, after getting as calm and thoughtful as she could about it, explain her thinking to her former husband, asking what he thought, and using him as a resource.

Not only did the divorced parents, in time, find that two heads could be more useful than one in thinking about their daughter's behavior but, in several months, Mrs. A was able to see that the relationship between herself and her ex-husband was working better. As a result, Mrs. A noted less depression in herself. She also noted that her relationship with her daughter worked much better. She could be more a parent, rather than fluctuating between boss and sibling. Her daughter's behavioral symptoms went away.

Many families have attested to the emotional relief they experience when they get in contact and maintain relationships with former spouses. Once calmer contact is re-established after the usual intensity and cutoff of the divorcing period, working toward separate boundaries, openness, and an equal stance become important here as in other relationships. Children of divorce who are lucky enough to have one parent working in this way show the positive effects.

The Single Life

> The degree of unresolved emotional attachment to parents is determined by the degree of unresolved emotional attachment each parent had in their own family of origin, the way their parents handled this in their marriage, the degree of anxiety during critical periods in life, and the way the parents handled this anxiety. The child is "programmed" into the emotional configuration very early in life, following which the amount of unresolved emotional attachment remains relatively fixed except for functional shifts in the parents . . . In broad terms, the amount of anxiety tends to parallel the degree of unresolved emotional attachment in the family.[12]

At high levels of differentiation, people can be comfortable in or out of relationships. But for those who end up single for large segments of their life either against their will or out of fear of attachments, nothing will be as useful to them as recognizing and working with their own emotional attachment to their parents.

There are very few people who do not have any relationships, even though they may be single. If they look around them, they will find that life is full of opportunities for relationships. Almost everyone has extended family relationships, friendships, and work relationships, all of which are available for work on self. If these relationships are taken as personal challenges, they can become fascinating projects in the differentiation of a self. Getting on with this work alleviates whatever discomfort that may arise from being without a spouse.

These relationships afford single people wonderful opportunities to work on furthering individuality without the distraction of an intense relationship. Navigating a single lifestyle from principles derived from the concept of differentiation of self makes for a productive and satisfying life course.

While married people may have to work to maintain an individual identity amid the togetherness of their lives, single people must sometimes work to provide enough relationships to test out their individuality. *It is only in relationship to emotional systems that one can differentiate a self.*

In single life the family of origin becomes again (or continues) as emotionally important. It is one's nuclear family. Single years provide time and opportunity to spend more time with one's family of origin, working toward differentiation of self. Family systems principles and a coach will be an invaluable guide in that effort.

Friendship systems are also extremely important to single people. A friendship system can provide some of the emotional groundedness that living in a nuclear family does. It can also provide a basis for differentiation of self when no family members are living or available.

Professional Relationships

> Terms such as "people," "person," and "family member" replaced the term "patient." Diagnoses were avoided, even in the therapist's private thinking. It has been more difficult to replace the concepts of "treatment," "therapy," and "therapist" and to modify the omnipotent position of the therapist to the patients. . . . Terms such as "supervisor," "teacher," and "coach" are probably best in conveying the connotation of an active expert coaching both individual players and the team to the best of their abilities.[13]

The professional/client relationship is at risk for all the relationship patterns. But it is especially vulnerable to the overfunctioning/

underfunctioning reciprocity. One person is asking for help in a problem situation. The other is trained to give help.

What is overfunctioning in the professional setting? How can the professional relate to people who have problems without overfunctioning?

The study (described in Chapter 16) of those fifteen people addicted to prescription medications taught the author much about the professional relationship. The addicted people initially appeared helpless, hopeless, and unable to cope without their medication. They were in a posture of underfunctioning in their primary relationships and had duplicated the pattern with their primary physicians, who, in an effort to be helpful, had prescribed the medicine, often in excess of recommended doses. In addition, this relationship posture was a repetition of an early-life relationship posture.

Underfunctioning behaviors observed in this group included whining, weeping, presentation of self as inadequate, hopeless, or "in a corner" with no options. Some of the overfunctioning characteristics the consultant learned to avoid were advising, over-teaching or knowing what someone else should think, preaching or knowing what someone else should do, and over helping to the point of overprescribing medications.

Initially, when the consultant interacted with people more as an equal who did not know all the answers, and put them more in charge of their own treatment with clear guidelines and parameters defined by the professional, some of them reacted negatively. But, when the guiding principles were explained, most people seemed to understand and were able to become more active on their own behalf. They came out of the victim posture when they took on responsibility as an active half of the treatment team.

Ideally, a professional can relate to and encourage a person's ability, focusing on their strengths and those of their families. The addicted person's presentation as hopeless, helpless, and weak was of a curiously demanding nature that actually belied tremendous strength. After all, they had succeeded in getting high doses of medications from other professionals, outside the limits of good medical practice. As the professional sees and relates to the assets of the person, the professional/client relationship is on the way toward becoming a relationship of equals.

The ideal professional/client relationship can be described the same way as any ideal relationship—separate, equal, and open. If the professional person is clear about their self boundaries and practiced at living within them, emotional neutrality will be easier. While the client may be looking intensely for a fused relationship in which he or she is in the underfunctioning position, the professional who knows about relationship patterns can resist, aiming for higher functioning in self in the bargain.

The professional can also learn about his or her own tendencies to overfunction which may, in fact, have been a factor in the choice of profession. Knowing one's own emotional process tendencies is, of course, the first step in learning to deal with them. In the case of overfunctioning, many professional people are functional if not actual oldests in their families of origin. As such, they often were given responsibility for the younger ones, whatever their sibling position.

How can a professional—an expert—relate to a client as an equal? Actually, the possession of skills, training, or knowledge need not create an unequal situation in a one-to-one relationship. A basic equality as humans can be recognized and assumed by the professional. Sometimes the professional's clients are children, as is the case with many teachers. But carrying the idea of promoting eventual equality in people can well serve these relationships and clients.

Openness in the professional relationship is useful, whether it be in the arena of medicine, nursing, therapy, education, the law, or any other profession. The more anxious the client, the more difficult it is to listen, but listening remains one of the most important skills a professional person can develop. Asking open questions rather than those that can be answered by "yes" or "no" will promote fuller explanations and the opportunity to listen with understanding. At best, professional responses are made from thinking rather than from emotion. Openness is not served by the professional who uses jargon specific to his or her discipline that the client does not understand.

Extraordinary Relationships

As we've seen, effective communication exists only to the degree that relationship patterns do not exist.

Even if the overfunctioning pitfall is avoided, other patterns can threaten the process, unless one is working on differentiation of self. Distance might show up in the form of the professional not answering calls or being vague. Conflict with a client turns up in a challenging or competitive communication style or in frequent disagreements. Triangling can be swift and automatic when other family members or agencies are drawn in. Cutoff occurs when the content of the work or the emotional process around it is not handled openly, or when someone perceives that the professional has lost neutrality, siding with one family member over another.

As with any other relationship, trading one relationship pattern for another solves nothing, although it is a universal and automatic human response. However, when principles of relationship theory are understood and used, especially when the professional is working toward a higher level of differentiation of self, management of the emotional self becomes more a priority and, with time, less difficult.

Workplace Relationships

> With an impersonal theory, it simply meant the focus was always on self instead of the other. This was used constantly in all administrative systems. When there was conflict or disharmony in the work system at Georgetown, it simply meant that self had played a part, and if self modified his part, the others would automatically change their part. The model has worked well through the years.[14]

Poorly functioning interpersonal relationships at work interfere with work output and cause more stress than any other single factor. While the primary emphasis in the workplace is, of course, the work itself, intensity in the workplace relationship system often means that personal competency and efficiency suffer, interfering with productivity.

Relationship principles apply in the workplace as they do in any other relationship system. When people spend a significant portion of time together, as they certainly do during a work week, they build up an emotional relationship system very similar to that of a family. It is not a family, and it is a mistake to refer to it as such, but emotions pass from one person to another and triangles and all the other relationship patterns can be seen. *All it takes to form an emotional system is to spend time together.*

The better the quality of the relationships in the workplace, the freer people are from expending energy and focus on relationship issues. The quality and quantity of the work improves. Work systems themselves operate at differing levels of differentiation, depending on the maturity levels of their leaders, the level of each individual in the organization and the amount of anxiety present at any given time. The higher the level of differentiation of the individuals, the more efficiently the workplace will run. Higher level leaders tend to attract and hire higher level people.

Unresolved relationship anxiety between leaders in the workplace filters down through the triangles of the system, finding expression several levels down in conflict, distance, or other patterned postures between individual workers. When that happens, repeated firings (which may become the order of the day in such a system) will be of no use. They will cease only when the leaders effectively work toward resolution of the unresolved anxiety in their own relationships with each other.

Theory points the way for management just as surely as for everyone else in the workplace. Managers, because of their leadership positions, have more influence on the system. If they keep in mind principles of differentiation, think systems, and work toward separate boundaries, equality, and openness, the entire workplace system will benefit.

After competence (for which there is no substitute*), relationships at work are the greatest single determinant of career success.* And here, too, family systems theory shows the way in managing self. Management of the self toward higher levels of functioning, and working toward emotionally calm contact in the workplace when everyone else is agitated, is valued. When one is relatively calm and in contact with others, the cerebral or thinking brain is not overburdened by anxiety generated in the emotional brain. Thus one is free to do better thinking about self-management as well as about the work itself. In other words, the ability to keep oneself relatively calm frees one to do better work. Excessive emotionality at work, far from solving anything, disrupts and interferes with getting the work done. The ability to choose emotional calm enhances the best functioning in any workplace.

In recent years, some workplace consultants have focused the organization on group ventilation of feelings, trying to ferret out the "problem people," rather than seeing process. This practice has led work groups into emotional chaos, with everyone thinking this kind of morass was somehow necessary to straighten out the emotional problems of various workplaces. Not only is such a process not necessary, it is counterproductive. Many workplaces have seen a meltdown following this type of emotions-based consultation process. When consultants focus instead on coaching leadership of an organization from a systems perspective, the leaders rise to the challenge. They are abundantly capable of addressing process in their organizations, given an adequate lens through which to see.

Staying in contact with as many important relationships as possible in the workplace system and using principles of good communications offers obvious benefits. Although relationship patterns will develop whenever anxiety increases, simply because they are so reflexive to the human, they can be seen more objectively by one who is aware of them. One objective person can stay a little more "out." This can lead to better functioning of the workplace triangles. In this way one becomes a valued individual in the work system. Communication principles based on knowledge of the relationship patterns become as applicable in the workplace as they are in any other emotional system.

Since people who spend a significant portion of time together eventually develop an emotional system similar to that of a nuclear family, it helps to know the sibling positions in their original families of the players in the system. This alone will often explain much about relationship events in the workplace. It also reveals much about the natural strengths of colleagues. This knowledge provides a bit of objectivity which makes it possible to take perceived problems less personally.

Because groups tend to assign what amounts to a "virtual" sibling position based on longevity, it is also helpful to know the approximate date that each person joined the system. The ones with most longevity are often treated as oldests in a family, and the last-to-come, as youngests. Understanding the relationship history of the system and knowing the established triangles of the emotional system of the workplace becomes invaluable as one attempts to be a part of the system. The more one knows about the history of the relationship system, the better able one is to emotionally handle one's self in it.

Places of work, like families, also go through periods of unusual stress, which tend to trigger relationship patterns and postures. Periods of unusual stress might include a transitional time around leadership changes, economic ups or downs, or reorganizations. As emotions intensify, it is more difficult for each individual to stay on course in the organization. It becomes tempting to be more in the triangles or polarized factions. But during a period of intense anxiety it remains a goal to work for emotional calm, staying in neutral contact with as many in the system as possible without taking sides, regardless of their emotionality or positions in factions.

If one continues, guided by inner principle, it is a differentiating position in the system. Added respect, promotions, and other rewards have been noted by some people who stayed on course with this kind of work for a significant period of time.

The efforts one makes in relationships at work have a beneficial effect on one's relationships outside of work. In the same way, increasing one's functioning in the family promotes one's functioning at work.

Leadership

> . . . If there was an emotional issue in the organization, I was
> playing a role in it, and if I could modify the part I was playing,
> the others would do the same. This principle has been used
> through the years in my own family, in my clinical work, and
> in my administrative functioning. Any time one key member
> of an organization can be responsibly responsible for self, the
> problem in the organization will resolve.[15]

> It is easy for a person in such a situation to say the situation is
> his "fault" and to accept the "blame" without being responsible.
> There is a fine line between accepting the responsibility for the
> part self plays in a situation and accepting the "blame" for it.[16]

Bowen theory is concerned with all areas of human behavior. As we
have seen, it is about relationships in the family and in other groups.
It is also a theory about leadership.

The leaders of the nuclear family are, of course, the parents. And,
just as families become a paradigm for understanding relationships
in all groups, parents become a paradigm for leadership in groups.
There are also other paradigms for leaders in the theory. One is the
automatic leadership people seem to acquire in their families as they
step up on the scale of differentiation of self. As they do that work,
they become better leaders in whatever groups they serve.

What is leadership in Bowen theory? Because individuals are at
different levels on the scale of differentiation, there is a possibility of
leadership functioning at a low level on the scale or at a higher level.
So, one goal is to endeavor to become a higher-level leader. That
takes place as people work on their personal level of differentiation
in their families of origin. Some of the work of going to a higher
level as a leader can be done in an organization. But it usually starts
in the family.

High-level leaders, as highly differentiated people, are guided
by principle, not by relationships or emotions. They take the time to

be clear and cognizant of their principles. They use them in guiding their behavior and in making decisions in their organizations. They assist their organizations to clarify guiding principles for it as well. High-level leaders are also relationship masters. They keep their relationships open, separate, and equal, no matter where they may be on the organization's chart.

When leaders of organizations in key positions begin and continue stepping up into the higher level that Bowen theory suggests, the whole organization benefits. If leaders of a society were to do the same, or should the society be fortunate enough to put into place some higher level leaders, the whole society would operate at a higher level of functioning. As Bowen theory becomes more a part of the general culture, one might expect leadership training based on it to become more in demand.

Societal Process and International Relationships

> The human is a narcissistic creature who lives in the present and who is more interested in his own square inch of real estate, and more devoted to fighting for his rights than in the multigenerational meaning of life itself. As the human throng becomes more violent and unruly, there will be those who survive it all. . . . I think the differentiation of self may well be one concept that lives into the future. . . . The future is limitless.[17]

The last concept to be added to Bowen theory is that of societal regression. It notes that, periodically, as anxiety begins to run higher in society, regressed behavior can be increasingly noted on a massive scale. A hallmark of such an anxious period is the unwillingness of families or other institutions of society (such as the court system) to take responsibility when behavior loses boundaries.

It is theorized that periods of regression alternate with periods of progression, in which responsibility in individuals, families, and societal institutions can be seen more readily. The alternating cycle is often referred to as *societal emotional process*. Periods of progression and better organization are presumed to occur at times of less societal anxiety.

Some triggers of societal anxiety at the present time might be overpopulation, lack of resources (perhaps related to the first problem), loss of contact with natural systems, environmental abuse, and the threats posed by man's possession of weapons of mass destruction. Violence such as terrorism and war are both products, as well as a further instigators, of anxiety and regression. The same can be said of irresponsible members of the media. As a societal regression develops, it is not only a marker of societal anxiety, but it also triggers further regression, in a vicious cycle.

Dr. Calhoun's Research

Dr. John B. Calhoun was a colleague of Dr. Bowen's at NIH. He worked with "universes" of mice who had all their needs supplied and were allowed unrestricted propagation. He found that when a rat or mouse population was allowed to breed for several generations in confined quarters, the anxiety resulting from overcrowding led to regressive behaviors. Males abandoned their usual guarding behaviors. Mothers forgot how to make effective nests, leaving the young exposed and vulnerable. As overcrowding progressed, females and males lost interest in one another. The females followed anything that moved, such as the experimenter himself. Males hung out in the periphery, useless and idle, endlessly grooming themselves and each other. Eventually procreation declined and the population decreased.[18]

In societal crisis, as in a family crisis, mounting anxiety moves intensely around triangles that become more and more evident. Polarized factions take the spotlight, promoting their emotionally-based positions and biased interpretations of the facts rather than trying to see the bigger picture or looking at the welfare of the larger society.

It seems clear that a societal regression is now taking place. A way of thinking that can inform human leadership at this time becomes more important than perhaps ever before.

If the world is to go from troubled and unpredictable international relations to those of a more durable and trustworthy nature, a new theory is needed to inform the thinking and movement of the political and diplomatic leaders of the world. In international relations, if leaders and countries can begin to make decisions that reflect an understanding of differentiation of self, acting responsibly from knowledge of facts and principle rather than reacting to and from the emotional process of society, *Homo sapiens* may survive the current regression.

Farren and Mulvihill[19] in *Paths to a Settlement in Northern Ireland*, interpret the resolution of the Northern Irish conflict through a Bowen theory lens of relationships, among others. They note that when England became neutral enough to side with neither of the Irish factions, but instead encouraged them to work it out by through the ballot box, and stayed in contact with the process as it unfolded, the conflict resolved itself. Such is the magic of a neutral angle in a triangle!

Most often the need in international relations is seen as one of conflict resolution. Many programs, conferences, grants, and organizations are designed with conflict resolution in mind. That is undoubtedly useful as far as it goes. War, after all, is conflict, but it is urgent that humans begin to consider how to minimize war on the planet. However, *conflict, important as it is, is only one of five relationship postures into which people and nations become locked.* For conflict to be understood and avoided, it would seem that all the postures will have to be understood and explored.

Negotiation experts have learned a great deal about managing the give and take of the negotiation process. Yet sometimes negotiations bog down, especially when it comes to having a way to think theoretically about *the relationships* between the negotiating parties themselves. Do the conflict management consultants have a way to think about managing their own emotionality?

Conferences where Bowen theory in international relations has been considered have been informative. Often audiences are quicker to see the applications internationally than in any other arena.

Extraordinary Relationships

Triangles of nations can frequently be recognized on newspapers' front pages. National negotiations often end up with other emotional postures. After all, these posturings, patterns, and decisions are the result of humans dealing with each other at negotiation tables. Other examples are obvious as well:

- War, of course, is conflict.
- Sanctions can be seen as conflict and distance (depending upon how much communication is taking place) and breaking of diplomatic relations as distance and/or cutoff.
- Throwing money at problems (i.e., financial aid that doesn't get to where it is most needed, but rather, goes to corrupt rulers) is incompetence and/or overfunctioning.
- Floundering in poverty and asking for bailouts instead of getting creative is an example of underfunctioning.

  Perhaps the most useful course now, is to ask questions:

- What would happen, at the academic level, if those who now are involved in the conflict resolution arena broadened their concerns to include the four other patterns where humans get stuck in their relationships—distance, cutoff, over- and underfunctioning and triangles?
- What if young negotiators-in-training were taught about the importance of managing themselves in the intensity?
- What part do the other patterns play in the kind of conflicts that lead ultimately to war?
- Short of war, how much human misery is bound up in these patterns? Do other patterns, other than conflict, lead to a kind of desperation that makes war seem a favorable outcome?
- If nations can be said to have postures, one to the other, what would a distant posture between two nations look like?
- How about overfunctioning/underfunctioning?
- Where do we see international triangling?

- Is a pattern of conflict between nations similar to or different from that in families?
- If the antidote to personal relationship patterning is moving on to a higher level of differentiation of self, can leaders/ negotiators begin to do that?
- Could high-level leadership raise the functioning level of an entire nation?
- Is it possible that a nation can be guided more by carefully considered principles than by its automatic reactivity?
- How clear are the principles of a nation? How do they get defined?
- How does a nation define its principles in the world?
- What is the difference between a nation whose actions in the world are led by principle and those whose actions are led by expediency?
- Do some nations exhibit a higher level of differentiation than others?[19]
- If violence erupts in the world, is there one principled response?
- Does a country with principles have an obligation where human rights are being violated?
- What would boundary violation and boundary setting look like?
- How does Bowen theory inform national leadership?
- If a leader were highly differentiated and moving on principle, would the nation move with him or her?

Bowen wrote the following on the subject:

> In a small or large social system, the move toward individuality is initiated by a single, strong leader with the courage of his conviction who can assemble a team and who has clearly defined principles on which he can base his decisions when the emotional opposition becomes anxious. The large social system goes through the same small steps with rebalancing the togetherness-individuality forces after each step. There is

never a threat of too much individuality. The human need for togetherness prevents going beyond a critical point. A society with higher levels of individuality provides great growth for individuals in the group, it handles anxiety well, decisions are based on principle and are easy, and the group is attractive to new members. This was characteristic of the United States for most of its history. The founders of the nation were strong on principles that provided flexible guarantees for individual rights and were attractive to immigrants from everywhere. The breakdown in individuality starts when leaders become lax in maintaining principles. When the next anxiety episode occurs, the leaders are sufficiently unsure of principles to begin making decisions based on the anxiety of the moment and the togetherness forces again become dominant.[20]

If the most influential segment of society could work toward the differentiation of self, it would automatically spread through the less influential segments and really benefit the less fortunate segment and raise the functional level of all society. The powerful togetherness forces in society oppose any efforts at differentiation of self. The lower the level of differentiation, the harder it is to start a differentiating effort. The togetherness forces at the present are intense. However, any differentiation in any key person in society automatically rubs off on others. Anyone who moves in this direction benefits society.[21]

Thinking It Over

The principles of Bowen theory amount to a guidebook that, if kept in mind, can be used at any time to address family, organizational, or even societal dilemmas.

Real Life Research

1. What are some of the factors that promote success in friendships?

2. In love relationships?

3. How does a calm marriage benefit the next generation?

4. What goes into not producing "child focused" children?

5. How are organizations emotionally like the family?

6. How are they different?

7. Why does divorce rarely solve anything?

8. Name some evidences of societal regression.

9. How would relationship principles derived from Bowen family systems theory help in international relations?

10. The list of questions on pages 202-203 could be considered for group discussion or in detail for individual thinking.

Endnotes

1. Bowen, Murray, *Family Therapy in Clinical Practice*, Jason Aronson, New York, 1978, p. 371.

2. Allman, John, *Evolving Brains*, Scientific American Library, New York, 1999, pp. 173-174.

3. Bowen, *op. cit.*, p. 530.

4. Bowen, *ibid.*, p. 373.

5. *Ibid.*, p. 540.

6. Bennett, W., *The Broken Hearth*, Doubleday, New York, 2002, p. 158.

7. Fischer, Helen, *The Anatomy of Love*, Norton, New York, 1992, p. 57.

8. Bowen, *op. cit.*, p. 297.

9. *Ibid.*, p. 535.

10. Beal, Edward, *Adult Children of Divorce*, Delacorte Press, 1991, p. 59.

11. Bowen, *op. cit.*, pp. 536–537.

12. *Ibid.*, pp. 309–310.

13. Bowen, Murray, in Kerr, Michael E. and Murray Bowen, *Family Evaluation,* W. W. Norton, New York, 1988, p. 373.

14. Please see the author's leadership trilogy: *Extraordinary Leadership, The Eight Concepts,* and *The Cornerstone Concept,* Leading Systems Press, Falls Church VA, for more on leadership based on Bowen family systems theory.

15. Bowen, Murray, *Family Therapy in Clinical Practice,* Jason Aronson, New York, 1978, p. 465.

16. *Ibid.,* p. 464.

17. *Ibid.,* p. 385.

18. Calhoun's work has been extensively observed and reported on by Dr. Roberta Holt in lectures at the Bowen Center for the Study of the Family.

19. Farren, Sean, and Mulvihill, Robert F., *Paths to a Settlement in Northern Ireland,* Oxford Press, New York, NY, 2000.

20. Katharine Baker has lectured on the subject at the Bowen Center for the Study of the Family.

21. Bowen, Murray, *Family Therapy in Clinical Practice,* Jason Aronson, New York, 1978, p. 279.

22. *Ibid.,* p.450.

EPILOGUE

The pursuit of extraordinary relationships as seen through the lens of Bowen family systems theory demonstrates anew the paradoxical nature of human existence. If one wants to work on a relationship, one must work on self. If one wants to work on individuality, it is best done in relationship to others. In order to be less distant, one must develop better boundaries. A thoughtful approach raises more questions than it answers and then jumps unhesitatingly into the paradoxes.

Most of the concepts introduced in this book have been presented in their simplest forms. A thorough understanding of Bowen theory will require further study. A thorough reading of Bowen's writing is necessary, as is rereading from time to time. Reading of the developing literature on the subject is highly recommended. But it is only a beginning.

It is not possible gain a thorough knowledge of Bowen theory by reading books. For a more thorough knowledge, including application to life, one will need a coach. But in some areas, consultants trained in Bowen family systems theory are few and far between. The number of trained professionals is growing, however. Established by Bowen himself is the training center in Washington, D.C., the Bowen Center for the Study of the Family.[1] It also maintains a list of professionals who have trained there. There are also centers for training in Chicago, Florida, Houston, Kansas City, Virginia and elsewhere. Some of these centers offer training as well as coaching for professionals and often, for anyone. Some of them can also help in locating a coach.

Professionals trained in Bowen theory often refer to the consulting process as "coaching" because so little of the useful work of self change actually occurs in the consulting room. It is done (like team sports) in the "field" of the family (instead of the arena).

Extraordinary Relationships

I believe the study of relationships to be the most important of human endeavors at the present time. If that study is not given high priority, our species may find itself on the way to extinction. Bowen theory is a useful inquiry into the science of relationships of all types, including, in my opinion, the troubled posturing and positioning of nation toward nation in the family of humankind.

At his funeral on October 20, 1990, I was honored to be able to read parts of the following thoughts from Dr. Bowen's writings:

> Man has overcome many of the forces that threatened his existence in former centuries. His life span has been increased by medical science, his technology has advanced rapidly, he has become increasingly more in control of his environment, which has been his adversary, and a higher percentage of the world's population has more economic security and creature comforts than at any time during man's history on earth. . . . By the late 1960's there was a hypothesis that has not only held up for several years, but that has also been strengthened by new evidence and the work of others. The hypothesis postulates that man's increasing anxiety is a product of population explosion, the disappearance of new habitable land to colonize, the approaching depletion of raw materials necessary to sustain life, and growing awareness that "spaceship earth" cannot indefinitely support human life in the style to which man and his technology have become accustomed. Man is a territorial animal who reacts to being "hemmed in" with the same basic patterns as the lower forms of life. Man tells himself other reasons to explain his behavior while important life patterns are the same as for non-thinking animals. Man has always used "getting away from the crowd" as a way of allaying anxiety and stabilizing his adjustment. The thesis here is that man became increasingly aware that his world is limited in size through rapid communication and television, and rapid travel. When animals are confined to a limited space and their numbers are increasing, they test the limits of the compound, there is more mobility

and moving around, and they finally come to live more in piles than spread evenly over existing space. Man has become more mobile the past twenty-five years, more people more often, and a higher percentage of the population is coming to live in the large metropolitan centers.

Another theoretical notion is important to this background thinking; it is another predictable characteristic of Man. With his logical thinking and knowledge, he could have known decades ago that he was on a collision course with his environment. His emotions, reactiveness, and its cause-and-effect thinking prevent him from really "knowing" what he could know. . . . Science has enabled Man to get beyond cause-and-effect thinking in many areas of life. He was first able to use systems in astronomy, far removed from him personally. Later he was able to "think systems" about the physical sciences, and later in the natural sciences. In the past decades, he has had some notion that systems thinking also applies to himself and his own emotional functioning, but in an emotional field, even the most disciplined systems thinker reverts to cause-and-effect thinking and to taking action based more on emotional reactiveness than objective thinking. This phenomenon plays an important part in man's decisions and actions about social problems.

Addendum for Second Edition

Twenty-six years after the first publication of *Extraordinary Relationships*, the world seems no closer to understanding human relationships than it was in 1992. Wars interminable, nations divided politically, families divorcing as frequently as ever, and murders in public places and much more are mundane in our world and demonstrate our lack of understanding.

There are many glimmers of hope, however, that Bowen family systems theory is becoming more widely appreciated. For example, the body of research in the field grows constantly. Bowen's work is cited more and more frequently in published articles and books. Wikipedia carries a biography of Bowen. *Family Systems*, the journal published by the Bowen Center for the Study of the Family, has become indexed, so that academicians can easily find articles it carried. Many books based in Bowen family systems theory have been published in the last twenty-six years, often with foreign translations. Bowen's collection of papers has recently been published in Spanish. Centers for teaching Bowen theory are increasing in the United States, and others have begun in Hong Kong, Taiwan, Sweden, and Australia. Individuals in many countries are using the theory in their own lives and work.

More and more, one hears phrases and words from the Bowen lexicon, like "triangles" or "boundaries" or even whole ideas that may have come from the Bowen library, are surfacing in everyday use over the popular media. In a tape, Bowen predicted that Bowen family systems thinking will bit by bit be slipped into use by the helping professions, and over time the whole of theory absorbed in that way.

It is a slow process, possibly because of the complexity of thinking systems. It does not come naturally to most of us. Whatever the case in the world at large, in the Bowen world there are many reasons to be encouraged that the word is getting out and lives are changing as a result of the new way of thinking about relationships in families, friendships and in organizations.

Endnote

1.   Website: www.thebowencenter.org

APPENDIX I

Glossary of Terms Used in Bowen Theory

Anxiety. Usually defined as the response of the organism to real or imagined threat. Clinical experience at different levels of differentiation of self suggests that anxiety is so continuously present in life, so much a fact of the individual's and family's patterns as to be stimulated in other ways as well. Anxiety can simply be "caught" from others even though there is no threat or imagined threat situation.

Another definition may therefore be proposed: *heightened reactivity*. Anxiety may be a reaction to stressors from outside the family system or the person, or it may be generated from inside the system, or from within the person. It may be chronic: passed along in a family system for years or even generations or it may be acute: relatively short-term. The effects of anxiety in a system are multiple: generally an increase of togetherness as evidenced by more triangling and other relationship postures. Physical, mental, emotional, or social symptoms of any intensity can occur at any level of differentiation, given enough anxiety carried long enough. Anxiety is also manifest in quantitative changes in the body that include cells, organs, and organ systems, as well as thought and behavioral expressions and patterns.

Basic Self. The differentiated or emotionally mature part of the self. It is guided by carefully thought-out principles that form an inner guidance system. Basic self is nonnegotiable. That is, it is not given up to other selves in relationships nor is it added to by other selves in a relationship. Therefore, its boundaries are "impermeable." It is distinguished from the pseudo (functional) self, which has more permeable boundaries, and can be added to or given up in relationships with the pseudo selves of others. The pseudo self functions better in favorable circumstances and less well in adverse conditions. Basic self, because of its inner guidance system and less permeable boundaries, is always more reliable for best thinking, decision-making, and directing behavior. People higher on the scale of differentiation have more basic self, whereas people lower on the scale have less basic self. Synonyms for basic self are solid self, differentiation of self, and individuality.

Differentiation of Self. As a noun, a way of thinking about the variation in functioning of humans and higher mammals. People all have differing abilities to adapt—that is, to deal with the exigencies of life, or live a goal-directed life of achievement. The word "differentiation" derives from the science of embryology. In the developing fetus, groups of cells that are identical in the beginning "differentiate" from each other in order to form the different organs of the body. People fall along a theoretical spectrum of differentiation—"the scale of differentiation of self"—according to their unresolved emotional attachments to their parents (and to some degree, their siblings). Some indices of differentiation include physical health and abilities, relationship success, intelligence, vocational success, reproduction, survival, and social skills. People range from very high levels of differentiation (theoretical "100") on the scale of self to very low levels (theoretical "0") on the scale, depending on how much basic self is present. People at higher levels, those with more basic self, tend toward more overall success in life, both vocationally and in their relationships. They also tend towards fewer physical, mental/ emotional or social symptoms. The more basic self a person attains, the more inner direction he or she has and the more choice at any given time regarding whether to operate out of emotions or intellect. People at higher levels function more out of their well thought-out principles than do people at lower levels.

People at lower levels have less choice between thinking and emotions. Their behavior patterns are more emotion-based and automatic. Emotion-based patterns include compliance, rebelliousness, fear of rejection, and fear of what others think; the automatic functions and responses of living things. Lower level individuals also have more attachment needs than do those at higher levels.

Differentiation of self has a rough equivalence with emotional maturity, though it has nothing to do with chronological age. It is a broader concept, taking in all the areas of functioning of an individual, including physical health.

The concept of differentiation of self contains a set of rather detailed principles which, when implemented, lead not only to improved emotional and relationship functioning, but also to improved functioning in all other spheres. Level of differentiation and amount of basic self are synonymous. At higher levels of differentiation, a greater amount of basic self exists, and at lower levels, a smaller amount.

As an action word, a verb, differentiation of self is the continued project of people who work with family systems theory on their relationship patterns, boundaries, communications, and emotional maturity.[1]

Emotional Maturity. The ability of the individual to manage the emotional part of the self in an adaptive way. In a more mature person, long term goals and benefits will be given priority over short term ones when they conflict. A similar concept to differentiation of self, it is not as inclusive. *(See also Differentiation of Self.)*

Emotional System. The emotional unit is a group of individuals who, by virtue of time spent together, are involved in meaningful relationships. This might include groupings in other species, the human family (nuclear or extended) or a workplace system. When individuals spend a significant amount of time together, sooner or later they will begin to trigger each other emotionally and the phenomenon of "passing" anxiety from one to another, in patterns, can be observed. Patterned emotional reactions include distance and cutoff, conflict, overfunctioning/underfunctioning, and triangling. These patterns are evidence of the fusions that exist in the emotional system. These phenomena are more pronounced the lower on the scale the group is and less so, the higher on the scale.

This term may also refer to the emotional system within an individual; that is, the part of the nervous system and organs involved in emotional responses. For instance, a perception of danger may involve sensory systems, such as hearing and vision, reptilian or limbic brain centers, the hypothalamus alerting the adrenals, the adrenal glands secreting adrenalin and cortisol, raising blood pressure and increasing cardiac output, as well as many other physiologic responses that make a fight or flight response possible.

Emotions. The instinctual or automatic processes that operate in animals and thus, in human beings. In Bowen family systems theory, even the heart and circulatory functions, digestion, and the endocrine system are included in emotional functioning. Other examples of emotional forces are territoriality and procreation, which are found in reptiles as well as more complex species, or nurturance of the young and play, which is found only in higher mammals. These reactions have an insistent quality. They originate in the various parts of the hindbrain and midbrain associated with these functions and are implemented by the individual's "emotional system," the brain/nervous system/end organs complex involved in the emotion. Emotions also include fight-or-flight reactions and patterned reactions, which become set in the developing organism with repetition.

Feelings. Emotions or automatic responses that are in awareness. They bridge automatic functions and responses to consciousness.

Fusion. Emotional attachment of two or more selves. The mother/child symbiosis is a paradigm but it can be seen in any intense important relationship. Both selves in a fusion are intensely emotionally reactive to each other. They often experience a loss or gain of self in the relationship.

Individuality Force. Synonymous with differentiation of self.

Inner Guidance System. *See Basic Self.*

Nuclear Family Emotional System. *See Emotional System.*

Pseudo Self. The immature or undifferentiated self that takes part in fusions—the giving or receiving of other selves in relationships. It is more reactive, less prone to think before acting, and not guided by thought-out principles. It is thus determined more by the environment, especially relationships, than by the self. It accepts unquestioningly data given by the culture or the family. Synonyms for pseudo self include the immature, functional, or undifferentiated, automatic self.

Reactivity. The tendency of the organism to respond to actual or perceived threat or the anxiety of others. It is more pronounced at lower levels of differentiation.

Scale of Differentiation of Self. An imaginary continuum (from theoretical "0" to theoretical "100") upon which all human beings fall, from the most differentiated to the least. A person may appear to function at a high level but if those in his or her emotional unit are not, he or she is probably gaining pseudo self from them, (gaining self at the expense of the functioning of others in the system) and so cannot be considered to actually possess the high level that is apparent.

Level of differentiation can be properly assessed only by observing an entire lifetime and by taking into consideration the levels of important others. The effects of circumstances and relationships show themselves in the pseudo self, not the basic self. *(See also Differentiation of Self.)*

Self. *See Basic Self.*

Symbiosis. A mutually dependent emotional attachment between two people. The concept comes from biology, where two organisms are dependent upon each other for survival. (The human, for example, lives in symbiosis with certain bacteria present in the gastrointestinal tract. The bacteria, being fed by the human's food, produce vitamin K, essential for the clotting of blood, and serve many other beneficial functions. In the family, individuals who fuse selves into relationships emotionally can be thought of as being in an emotional symbiosis.

To the degree that the symbiosis is resolved, or grown away from, during maturation, the individual is said to have differentiated a self. To the degree that the original tendency toward symbiosis remains in place, differentiation of self is incomplete and the self is vulnerable to forming other emotionally dependent relationships.

System. *See Emotional System.*

Togetherness Force. The tendency of organisms under threat or in an anxious environment to lose self to the group. Synonyms include: undifferentiation, symbiosis, and immaturity.

Triangle. Three individuals emotionally related to each other start to pass their anxiety to each other, or "triangle." Triangles are the building blocks of emotional systems. Emotional intensity takes place alternately among the different pairs forming the triangle, thus anxiety travels around it. In each family system there are many triangles, some of which reach out to society at large by way of friendship systems or agencies of society. In this way, society itself is built of interlocking triangles.

Endnote

1. The useful distinction between differentiation as noun and as verb was first made by Kathleen Kerr in lectures and comments at the Bowen Center.

APPENDIX II

The Eight Concepts of Bowen Theory

This summary of Bowen family systems theory first appeared in *Connecting with our Children*[1]. *The Eight Concepts of Bowen Theory*[2] is also recommended as a beginner's primer on Bowen family systems theory.

Concept 1: Nuclear Family Emotional System

The nuclear family as an emotional unit, rather than the individual, is the idea most fundamental to all the other concepts. It is basic to "thinking systems." No one had seen it before Bowen.

When people live together in a family they tend to pass anxiety and immaturity from one person to another. *As anxiety automatically moves in relationship systems it often does so in well-defined and often-observed ways.* These become relationship "postures" (if used short-term) or "patterns" (if used long term). The specific patterns characteristic of an emotional system are:

- Conflict
- Distance and Cutoff
- Overfunctioning/underfunctioning reciprocity
- Triangling

Each is adopted in order to manage relationship anxiety. However, when employed excessively and habitually they trigger anxiety of their own. The movement of anxiety and immaturity between people who are important to one another can also be described as donating or taking self to and from each other.

Concept 2: Scale of Differentiation of Self

The scale of differentiation of self refers to a theoretical scale that separates people along a continuum, from zero to one hundred, according to their ability to adapt over a lifetime. More differentiated people do well in most areas. Less differentiated people do less well. *The basic reason for this difference concerns how people function emotionally in relationships, derived from years of functioning in their families of origin, their formative relationship system.* This can be estimated roughly but never accurately measured, since that would involve looking at an entire lifetime. The way we function in relationships is built into us by the time we leave home and determines our comfort in, dependence on, and success in, relationships. At the higher end of the scale people are freer from emotionally fusing into relationships. They are more comfortable and successful. This relationship freedom promotes success in all other areas of life— vocational, social, mental/emotional/brain functioning, as well as physical health. People higher on the scale have more individuality life force, (basic self) and less togetherness life force (tendency to fuse into relationships).

At the lower levels on the scale, the relationship fusions make for less satisfaction and stability in life. Anxiety at the lower end of the scale is higher and functioning is lower in all areas (social, mental/ emotional/brain/physical).

How we function in relationships actually affects the brain and how it handles thinking and emotions. At the higher end of the scale there is more choice between the intellectual system and the emotional/feeling system and at the lower end there is little or no choice. Because thinking is clearer for people at the high end of the scale, *their well thought-out principles act as an inner guidance system.*

Concept 3: Triangles

The triangle is the most stable small unit of emotional systems. In groups of people, anxiety routes itself around this "molecule" of human interaction. Triangles connect small and large systems by building on themselves and interlocking. Thus all of society itself is ultimately made up of triangles. Triangles are so important that they appear in most of the eight concepts.

When two people have a problem in their interactions, a third is often attracted or drawn in by the original twosome. The focus on a child is an example of a triangle, where parents, ignoring their unresolved anxiety, allow it to become directed at a child. In a patterned way, the family anxiety then flows automatically toward the child. This process can result in a symptomatic child. "Triangling" can result in insiders and outsiders, with two agreeing the other is "the problem" or is "wrong" about something.

Concept 4: Cutoff

The most extreme form of relationship distance is called cutoff. Cutoff proceeds from unresolved emotional attachment and occurs when people significant to one another discontinue contact with, or interest in, one another. It produces extreme effects in the form of poor relationships in other areas of life. It also leads to emotional, physical, or social symptoms. Cutoff is produced by extreme emotional intensity that one or both parties ultimately find intolerable.

Concept 5: Family Projection Process

The family emotional process, through its fusions, affects some of the offspring more than others. Because of that, the members of a nuclear family do not end up with the same level of differentiation even though the two parents are at the same level. In this way, anxiety is off-loaded to children in a family in differing amounts. Some get less focus and anxiety, leaving them with more maturity, while some receive more focus and anxiety, leaving them with greater immaturity. By the time people leave their families of origin, their level of differentiation is permanent, all things being equal. Because of the different levels of differentiation of self in different siblings, their life courses may be quite different.

Concept 6: Multigenerational Transmission Process

Because of the family projection process, anxiety and immaturity travel through the generations of a family. When the generations of a family are studied in framework of family systems theory, the importance of movement of immaturity through the emotional currents of the family's generations can be seen in family stressors, themes, and differences in functioning in different branches of a family. Trends in functioning upward or downward through branches of a family can be observed.

Concept 7: Sibling Position and Functioning Position

One of the stronger determinants of one's functional position in a family, sibling position is described by both age rank and gender configuration in the research of Dr. Walter Toman. Sibling position often sheds a great deal of light on the relationship puzzle. It can be a strong factor in determining personality. Combinations of sibling positions in relationships can often predict both relationship strengths and challenges for the relationship. Sibling position, family projection process, and multigenerational transmission process combine to create *functional positions* that tend to stay with people throughout their lives.

Concept 8: Societal Emotional Process

Societal emotional process describes the periods of chaos, disorderliness, and irresponsibility that occur in society at times of greater anxiety, as well as the more orderly periods of less anxiety. It was originally called "societal regression." It is unclear what triggers the societal anxiety that leads to periods of regression. Many triggers have been suggested such as overpopulation, weapon threats, lack of leadership, economic threat, and decreasing availability of land and other resources. These may all have the common denominator of threat to survival.

Endnotes

1. Gilbert, Roberta, *Connecting With Our Children*, John Wiley and Sons, New York, NY, 1999 Part II, pp. 61 ff.

2. Gilbert, Roberta, *The Eight Concepts of Bowen Theory*, Leading Systems Press, Falls Church, VA, 2006.

APPENDIX III

Differentiation of Self in Bowen's Words

Dr. Bowen wrote several times of the differences in lives lived at different levels on the hypothetical scale of differentiation. Here is one of his descriptions, written in 1971.

"Differentiation of Self Scale." This scale is a way of evaluating all people on a single continuum, from the lowest to the highest possible level of human functioning. The scale ranges from 0 to 100 . . .

"At the lowest point on the scale is the lowest possible level of self or the greatest degree of no-self or undifferentiation. At the highest point on the scale is a postulated level of complete differentiation of perfect self, which man has not yet achieved. The level of differentiation is the degree to which one self fuses or merges into another self in a close emotional relationship. The scale eliminated the concept of normal, which has been elusive for psychiatry.

"The scale has nothing to do with emotional illness or psycho-pathology. There are low-scale people who manage to keep their lives in emotional equilibrium without developing emotional illness, and there are higher-scale people who can develop sever symptoms under great stress. However, lower-scale people are vulnerable to stress and are much more prone to illness, including physical and social illness, and their dysfunction is more likely to become chronic when it does occur. Higher-scale people can recover emotional equilibrium quickly after the stress passes.

"Two levels of self have been postulated. One is solid self, make up of firmly held convictions and beliefs. It is formed slowly and can be changed from within self, but it is never changed by coercion or persuasion by others. The other level of self is the pseudo-self, made up of knowledge incorporated by the intellect and of principles and beliefs acquired from others. The pseudo-self is acquired from others, and it is negotiable in relationship with others. It can be changed by emotional pressure to enhance one's image with others or to oppose the other.

"In the average person, the level of solid self is relatively low in comparison with the level of pseudo-self. A pseudo-self can function well in most relationships. But in an intense emotional relationship, such as marriage, the pseudo-self of one merges with the pseudo-self of the other. One becomes the functional self and the other a functional no-self. The emotional interplay in fusion states, the undifferentiated family ego mass, is the subject of the dynamics in a family emotional system.

"Low-scale people live in a feeling world in which they cannot distinguish feeling from fact. So much life energy goes into seeking love or approval or in attacking the other for not providing it that there is no energy for developing a self or for goal-directed activity. The lives of low-scale people are totally relationship-oriented. Major life decisions are based on what feels right. A low-scale person with a life in reasonable asymptomatic adjustment is one who is able to keep the feeling system in equilibrium by giving and receiving love and by the sharing of self with others. Low-scale people do so much borrowing and trading of self and show such wide fluctuations in their functioning levels of self that it is difficult to estimate their basic levels of self except over long periods of time.

"As a group, low-scale people have a high incidence of human problems. Relationships are tenuous, and a new problem can arise in an unsuspected area even while they are trying to deal with the previous problem. When the relationship equilibrium fails, the family goes into functional collapse, with illness or other problems. They can be too numb to feel, and there is no longer any energy to seek love and approval. So much energy is devoted to the discomfort of the moment that they live from day to day. At the very lowest point on the scale are those too impaired to live outside an institution.

"People in the 25-50 segment of the scale also live in a feeling-dominated world, but the fusion of selfs is less intense, and there is increasing capacity to differentiate a self. Major life decisions are based on what feels right rather than on principle, much life energy goes into seeking love and approval, and there is little energy for goal-directed activity.

"Those in the 35-40 range present some of the best examples of a feeling-oriented life. They are removed from the impairment and life paralysis that characterize the lower-scale people, and the feeling orientation is more clearly seen. They are sensitized to emotional disharmony, to the opinions of others, and to creating a good impression. They are apt students of facial expressions, gestures, tones of voice, and actions that may mean approval or disapproval. Success in school or at work is determined more by approval from important others than by the basic value of the work. Their spirits can soar with expressions of love and approval or be dashed by the lack of it. These are people with low levels of solid self but reasonable levels of pseudo-self, which is obtained from and is negotiable in the relationship system.

"People in the upper part of the 25-50 segment of the scale have some awareness of intellectual principles, but the system is still so fused with feeling that the budding self is expressed in dogmatic authoritativeness, in the compliance of a disciple, or in the opposition of a rebel. Some of those in this group use intellect in the service of the relationship system. As children, their academic prowess won them approval. They lack their own convictions and beliefs, but they are quick to know the thoughts and feelings of others, and their knowledge provides them with a facile pseudo-self. If the relationship system approves, they can be brilliant students and disciples. If their expectations are not met, they assemble a pseudo-self in point by point opposition to the established order.

"People in the 50-60 segment of the scale are aware of the difference between feelings and intellectual principle, but they are still so responsive to the relationship system that they hesitate to say what they believe, lest they offend the listener.

"People still higher on the scale are operationally clear about the differences between feelings and intellect, and they are free to state beliefs calmly, without attacking the beliefs of others for the enhancement of self and without having to defend themselves against the attacks of others. They are sufficiently free of the control of the feeling system to have a choice between intimate emotional closeness and goal-directed activity, and they can derive satisfaction and pleasure from either. They have a realistic appraisal of self to others, in contrast to lower-scale people, who feel self to be the center of the universe and who either overvalue or devalue self.

"The differentiation of self scale is important as a theoretical concept for viewing the total human phenomenon in perspective. It is valuable in estimating the over-all potential of people and in making predictions about the general pattern of their lives. But it is not useful in making month to month or even year to year evaluations of scale levels. There is so much trading and borrowing and negotiating for pseudo-self in the relationship system, especially in the lower half of the scale, and such wide functional shifts in the level of self that it is difficult to estimate scale levels on short term information.

"Most people spend their lives at the same basic level they had when they left their parental families. They consolidate this level in a marriage, after which there are few life experiences that change this basic level. Many life experiences automatically raise or lower the functioning levels of self, but this shift can be as easily lost as gained. There are calculated ways to raise the basic level of self, but doing so is a monumental life task, and it is easy to say that the possible gain is not worth the effort. The method of psychotherapy described here is directed at helping families differentiate a few points higher on the scale."

In 1972 Bowen wrote:

"People in the lower half of the scale live in a 'feeling' controlled world in which feelings and subjectivity are dominant over the objective reasoning process most of the time. They do not distinguish feelings from fact and major life decisions are based on what 'feels' right. Primary life goals are oriented around love, happiness, comfort, and security: these goals come closest to fulfillment when relationships with others are in equilibrium. So much life energy goes into seeking love and approval, or in attacking the other for not providing it, that there is little energy left for self-determined, goal-directed activity. . . . An important life principle is 'giving and receiving' love, attention, and approval. Life can stay in symptom-free adjustment as long as the relationship system is in comfortable equilibrium. Discomfort and anxiety occur with events that disrupt or threaten the relationship equilibrium. Chronic disruption of the relationship system results in dysfunction and a high incidence of human problems, including physical and emotional illness and social dysfunction. People in the upper half of the scale have an increasingly defined level of basic self and less pseudo-self. Each person is more of an autonomous self: there is less emotional fusion in close relationships, less energy is needed to maintain self in the fusions, more energy is available for goal-directed activity, and more satisfaction is derived from directed activity. Moving into the upper half of the scale, one finds people who have an increasing capacity to differentiate between feelings and objective reality. For instance, people in the 50-to-75 range of the scale have increasingly defined convictions and opinions on most essential issues but they are still sensitive to opinions of those about them and some decisions are based on feelings in order not to risk the disapproval of important others.

"According to the theory, there is some degree of fusion in close relationships, and some degree of an 'undifferentiated family ego mass' at every scale level below 100. When the scale was first devised, the 100 level was reserved for the being who was perfect in all levels of emotional, cellular, and physiological functioning. I expected there might be some unusual figures in history, or possibly some living persons who would fit into the mid-90 range. Increasing experience with the scale indicates that all people have areas of good functioning and essential areas in which life functioning is poor . . .

my impression is that 75 is a very high-level person and that those above 60 constitute a small percentage of society.

"The characteristics of high-scale people convey an important aspect of the concept. They are operationally clear about the difference between feeling and thinking. . . . The relative separation of feelings and thinking brings life much more under the control of deliberate thoughts, in contrast to low-scale people whose life is a pawn of the ebb and flow of the emotional process. In relationships with others, high-scale people are free to engage in goal-directed activity, or to lose 'self' in the intimacy of a close relationship, in contrast to low-scale people who either have to avoid relationships lest they slip automatically into an uncomfortable fusion, or have no choice but continued pursuit of a close relationship for gratification of emotional 'needs.' The high-scale person is less reactive to praise or criticism and he has a more realistic evaluation of his own self in contrast to the lower-level person whose evaluation is either far above or far below reality. . . .

". . . A detailed history of functional shifts within a family over a period of years can convey a fairly accurate pattern of the family members in relation to each other . . . . The life style of a person at one level is so different from someone only a few points removed on the scale that they do not choose each other for personal relationships. There are many life experiences that can raise or lower the *functioning* levels of self, but few that can change the basic level of differentiation acquired while people are still with their parental families. Unless there is some unusual circumstance, the basic level from their parental family is consolidated in a marriage, following which the only shift is a functional shift. The functional shits can be striking. For example, a wife who had a functional level at marriage equal to her husband's may become de-selfed to the point of chronic alcoholism. She then functions far below her original level while the husband functions equally far above his original level. Many of these functional levels are sufficiently consolidated so that they can appear much like basic levels to the inexperienced."

By 1976, the concept was fleshed out even further:

"At the fusion end of the spectrum, the intellect is so flooded by emotionality that the total life course is determined by the emotional process . . . rather than beliefs or opinions. The intellect exists as an appendage of the feeling system. It may function reasonably well in mathematics or physics, or in impersonal areas, but on personal subjects its functioning is controlled by the emotions. The emotional system is hypothesized to be part of the instinctual forces that govern automatic functions. The human is adept at explanations to emphasize that he is different from lower forms of life. The more a life is governed by the emotional system, the more it follows the course of all instinctual behavior, in spite of intellectualized explanations to the contrary. At higher levels of differentiation, the function of the emotional and intellectual systems are more clearly distinguishable. There are the same automatic emotional forces that govern instinctual behavior, but intellect is sufficiently autonomous for logical reasoning and decisions based on thinking. When I first began to present this concept, I used the term *undifferentiated family ego mass* to describe the emotional 'stuck togetherness' in families Although this phrase was an assemblage of words from conventional theory, and thus did not conform to the plan to use concepts consistent with biology, it fairly accurately described emotional fusion. . . .

"The most common criticism was that a differentiated person appeared to be cold, distant, rigid, and nonfeeling. It is difficult for professional people to grasp the notion of differentiation when they have spent their working lives believing that the free expression of feelings represents a high level of functioning and intellectualization represents an unhealthy defense against it. . . . A poorly differentiated person is trapped within a feeling world. . . . A segment of these . . . people use random, inconsistent, intellectual-sounding verbalization to explain away their plight. A more differentiated person can participate freely in the emotional sphere without the fear of becoming too fused with others. He is also free to shift to calm, logical reasoning for decisions that govern his life. The logical intellectual process is quite different from the inconsistent, intellectualized verbalizations of the emotionally fused person. . . .

". . . The schematic framework and the use of the term scale resulted in hundreds of letters requesting copies of 'the scale.' Most who wrote had not grasped the concept nor the variables that govern the functional levels of differentiation. . . . The theoretical concept is most important. It eliminates the barriers between schizophrenia, neurosis, and normal: it also transcends categories such as genius, social class, and cultural-ethnic differences. It applies to all human forms of life. It might even apply to subhuman forms if we only knew enough. . . .

". . . In periods of emotional intimacy, two pseudo-selfs will fuse into each other, one losing self to the other, who gains self. The solid self does not participate in the fusion phenomenon. The solid self says, 'This is who I am, what I believe, what I stand for, and what I will do or will not do,' in a given situation. The solid self is made up of clearly defined beliefs, opinions, convictions, and life principles. These are incorporated into self from one's own life experiences, by a process of intellectual reasoning and the careful consideration of the alternatives involved in the choice. . . . Each belief and life principle is consistent with all the others, and self will take action on the principles even in situations of high anxiety and duress. . . .

"The pseudo-self is created by emotional pressure, and it can be modified by emotional pressure. Every emotional unit, whether it be the family or the total of society, exerts pressure on group members to conform to the ideals and principles of the group. The pseudo-self is composed of a vast assortment of principles, beliefs, philosophies, and knowledge acquired because it is required or considered right by the group. Since the principles are acquired under pressure, they are random and inconsistent with one another, without the individual's being aware of the discrepancy. Pseudo-self is appended onto the self, in contrast to solid self which is incorporated into self after careful, logical reasoning. The pseudo-self is a 'pretend' self. It was acquired to conform to the environment and it contains discordant and assorted principles that pretend to be in emotional harmony with a variety of social groups, institutions, businesses, political parties, and religious groups, without self's being aware that the groups are inconsistent with each other. The joining of groups is motivated more by the relationship system than the principle involved. . . . The solid self is intellectually aware of the inconsistency between the groups, and the decision to join or reject membership is an intellectual process based on careful weighing of the advantages and disadvantages.

"The pseudo-self is an actor and can be many different selfs. The list of pretends is extensive. He can pretend to be more important or less important, stronger or weaker, or more attractive or less attractive than is realistic. . . . The level of solid self is stable. The pseudo-self is unstable, and it responds to a variety of social pressures and stimuli. The pseudo-self was acquired at the behest of the relationship system, and it is negotiable in the relationship system. . . .

". . . I believe that the level of solid self is lower, and of the pseudo-self . . . higher in all of us than most are aware. It is the pseudo-self that is involved in fusion and the many ways of giving, receiving, lending, borrowing, trading, and exchanging of self. In any exchange, one gives up a little self to the other, each is trying to be the way the other wants self to be, and each in turn makes demands on the other to be different. This is pretending and trading in pseudo-self. In a marriage, two pseudo-selfs fuse into a we-ness in which one becomes the dominant decision maker or the most active in taking initiative for the we-ness. The dominant one gains self at the expense of the other, who loses it. The adaptive one may volunteer to give up self to the dominant one, who accepts it: or the exchange may be worked out after bargaining. The more the spouses can alternate these roles, the healthier the marriage. The exchanging of selfs may be on a short- or long-term basis. The borrowing and trading of selfs may take place automatically in a work group in which the emotional process ends up with one employee in the one-down or de-selfed position, while the others gain self. This exchange of pseudo-self is an automatic emotional process that occurs as people manipulate each other in subtle life postures. The exchanges can be brief—for instance, criticism that makes one feel bad for a few days: or it can be a long-term process in which the adaptive spouse becomes so de-selfed, he or she is no longer able to make decisions and collapses in selfless dysfunction—psychosis or chronic illness. These mechanisms are much less intense in better levels of differentiation or when anxiety is low, but the process of people losing and gaining self in an emotional network is so complex and the degree of shifts so great that it is impossible to estimate functional levels of differentiation except from following a life pattern over long periods.

"Profile of low levels of differentiation . . . .they say 'I feel that . . ."* when it would be accurate to express an opinion or belief. They consider it truthful and sincere to say 'I feel,' and false and insincere to express an opinion from themselves. They spend their lives in a day to day struggle to keep the relationship system in balance, or in an effort to achieve some degree of comfort and freedom from anxiety. They are incapable of making long-term goals except in vague terms, such as 'I want to be successful, or happy, or have a good job, or have security.' They grow up as dependent appendages of their parents, following which they seek other equally dependent relationships in which they can borrow enough strength to function. A no-self person who is adept at pleasing his boss may make a better employee than one who has a self. This group is made up of people preoccupied with keeping their dependent relationships in harmony, people who have failed and who go from one symptomatic crisis to another, and people who have given up in the futile effort to adapt. . . .

"Profile of moderate levels of differentiation of self. . . . life styles are more flexible than the lower levels of differentiation. When anxiety is low, functioning can resemble that of low levels of differentiation. Lives are relationship oriented, and major life energy goes to loving and being loved, and seeking approval from others. Feelings are more openly expressed than in lower level people. Life energy is directed more to what others think and to winning friends and approval than to goal-directed activity. Self esteem is dependent on others. It can soar to heights with a compliment or be crushed by

criticism. Success in school is oriented more to learning the system and to pleasing the teacher than to the primary goal of learning. Success in business or in social life depends more on pleasing the boss or the social leader, and more on who one knows and gaining relationship status than in the inherent value of the work . . . . Lacking a solid self-conviction about the world's knowledge, they use pseudo-self statements, such as 'The rule says . . .' or 'Science has proved . . .' taking information out of context to make their points. They may have enough free-functioning intellect to have mastered academic knowledge about impersonal things. . . . However, intellect about personal matters is lacking and their personal lives are in chaos.

"The pseudo-self may be a conforming disciple who pretends to be in harmony with a particular philosophy or set of principles or, when frustrated, he can assume the opposite posture as a rebel or revolutionary person. The rebel is lacking a self of his own. His pseudo-self posture is merely the exact opposite of the majority viewpoint. The revolutionary person is against the prevailing system, but he has nothing to offer in its place. The sameness of polarized opposites in emotional situations has led me to define revolution as a convulsion that prevents change. It is a relationship-oriented energy that goes back and forth on the same points, the issue of each side being determined by the position of the other: neither is capable of a position not determined by the other.

"People in the moderate range of differentiation have the most intense versions of overt feeling. . . . They are in a lifelong pursuit of the ideal close relationship. When closeness is achieved, it increases the emotional fusion to which they react with distance and alienation, which can then stimulate another closeness cycle. Failing to achieve closeness, they may go to withdrawal and depression, or to pursuit of closeness in another relationship. . . .

*"**Profile of moderate to good differentiation of self.** These* are the people with enough basic differentiation between the emotional and intellectual systems for the two systems to function alongside each other as a cooperative team. The intellectual system . . . can hold its

own and function autonomously without being dominated by the emotional system when anxiety increases. [A person functioning at levels] above 50 . . . has learned that the emotional system runs an effective course in most areas of functioning, but in critical situations the automatic emotional decisions create long-term complications for the total organism. People above 50 have developed a reasonable level of solid self on most of the essential issues in life. In periods of calm, they have employed logical reasoning to develop beliefs, principles, and convictions that they use to overrule the emotional system in situations of anxiety and panic. . . . People at the lower part of this group are those who know there is a better way; but . . . they end up following life courses similar to those below 50.

"People in the upper part of this group are those in whom there is more solid self . . . no longer a prisoner of the emotional-feeling world. They are able to live more freely and to have more satisfying emotional lives within the emotional system. They can participate fully in emotional events knowing they can extricate themselves with logical reasoning when the need arises. There may be periods . . . in which they permit the automatic pilot of the emotional system to have full control, but when trouble develops they can take over, calm the anxiety, and avoid a life crisis. . . . They are not unaware of the relationship system, but their life courses can be determined more from within themselves than from what others think. . . . They marry spouses with equal levels of differentiation. The lifestyle of a spouse at another level would be sufficiently different to be considered emotionally incompatible. The marriage is a functioning partnership. The spouses can enjoy the full range of emotional intimacy without either being de-selfed by the other. They can be autonomous selfs together or alone. . . . Spouses . . . can permit their children to grow and develop their own autonomous selfs without undue anxiety or without trying to fashion their children in their own images. The spouses and the children are each more responsible for themselves, and do not have to blame others for failures or credit anyone else for their successes. People with better levels of differentiation are able to function well with other people, or alone, as the situation may require. Their lives are more orderly, they are able to cope successfully with a broader range of human situations, and they are remarkable free from the full range of human problems. . . .

". . . A common mistake is to equate the better differentiated person with a 'rugged individualist.' I consider rugged individualism to be the exaggerated pretend posture of a person struggling against emotional fusion. The differentiated person is always aware of others and the relationship system around him. There are so many forces and counterforces and details in differentiation that one has to get a broad panoramic view of the total human phenomenon in order to be able to see differentiation. Once it is possible to see the phenomenon, there it is, operating in full view, right in front of our eyes. Once it is possible to see the phenomenon, it is then possible to apply the concept to hundreds of different human situations. To try to apply it without knowing it is an exercise in futility."

APPENDIX IV

Toman's Sibling Postion Portraits

Following is a condensed version of the sibling-position portraits as Dr. Water Toman originally described them.

It should be noted, also, that much of personality development has to do with one's parents' sibling positions. The parents' personality characteristics, in large part derived from their own sibling positions, become important determining factors in personality development. The way parents relate to their children has a great deal to do with the relationships they formed with their siblings. For example, a youngest brother of brothers, as a father, may tend to relate more easily to his older son who is an older brother of brothers, just as he had at an earlier in his life related to his own older brother. This relationship will then have a bearing on his oldest son's personality development, and will possibly be a different relationship than the father will have with his other children. The personality development of all siblings will be differentially affected by their parents' sibling position. This is part of the answer to the question, "How can people reared by the same parents turn out so differently?"

- *In trying to determine characteristics of individuals in the middle of a large family, see "the Middle Child" [p. 241] for an explanation of how to use this guide.*

The Oldest Brother of Brothers

The oldest brother of bothers finds it easy to assume responsibility for other people, especially men. He is nurturing and caring of the groups he assumes responsibility for and expects loyalty and trust in return. He accepts authority easily, but may become bossy. He easily knows and implements the ingredients of achievement. He is sensitive and shy around women. He is attracted to the youngest sister of either brothers or sisters. An oldest sister of brothers could also please him if she does not mother him. An oldest sister of sisters would be a difficult match for him because of her similar tendency to lock horns when it comes to leadership. He is most likely to choose women of the same sibling position as that of his mother. His marriage will do better if he is permitted to maintain male friendships. He is a concerned and responsible father if he does not become too strict, controlling, or uninvolved. He will tend to have friendships among several sibling positions, but may clash with friends who are also older brothers.

The Youngest Brother of Brothers

The youngest brother of brothers is more of a follower and leans especially on men. He works well with men who appreciate and respect him and enjoys being understood by other men. He does not really enjoy being a leader. He may be obstinate, daring, bold, and complaining. Physically strong, he is kind-hearted and soft. He is not as interested in achievement and acquisition as in quality of life and the joys of the moment. He is not goal or content oriented but if not tied to routine work he may accomplish great and unusual things, especially in scientific, technical, or artistic fields. With women he is soft, yielding, and faithful, if unpredictable. His best partner would be the older sister of brothers or sisters or the youngest sister of brothers. His poorest match would be with the youngest sister of sisters or an only child. He too will want to continue contact with his male friends. He is a good companion to his children, as a father, but may tend to relate in the family too much as a child. Best friends tend to become oldest brothers of brothers or middle brothers who had younger brothers or only children whose fathers were oldest siblings.

Oldest Brother of Sisters

The oldest brother of sisters understands, appreciates, and works well with women. He does not refuse leadership roles but also does not seek them out. He is not susceptible to male chauvinism and is not one to join male clubs. He is not obsessed with work, maintaining a live-and-let-live philosophy. Materialism is not one of his vices. He will make sacrifices for the woman in his life. His best partner would be the youngest sister of brothers. The oldest sister of brothers may mother him too much, and he shows little attraction for oldest sisters of sisters. He is a good father, concerned about his children, and willing to be actively involved with them, but he does not become consumed with worry over his children since, to him, his wife is the most important person in the family. Male friends interest him little and in groups he is somewhat neutral and detached.

Youngest Brother of Sisters

The youngest brother of sisters, without trying, attracts solicitation, care, and services from women around him. He was valued and privileged by his parents, and he tends to keep that position as he goes through life in his relationships at work and in the family. He can assume leadership roles easily, especially with feminine support, but his male colleagues are skeptical. He has a well-developed ability to charm women but really doesn't understand them, feeling he himself is all that they should really need. His best partner is an older sister of brothers. An oldest sister of sisters seems self-righteous and strict to him. A youngest sister of brothers seems not motherly enough and too dependent. A youngest sister of sisters seems too impulsive and ambitious. He is not especially keen to be a father but indulges his wife her wishes. He may experience some jealousy of his wife's attention to the children. He is both companion and advisor to the children. He may tend to grant them too much freedom and independence. He is less interested in male friends than other men.

Male Only Child

The male only child is used to living with considerably older people and tends to prefer having older people around him throughout his life, wanting to be loved, nurtured, and supported by them. He is quite convinced of his own importance in the scheme of things. Because he received more attention and stimulation from his parents than other children, as a rule he usually had an edge in intelligence and talent as he was growing up. That edge, combined with encouragement from parents, guardians, and teachers may stimulate him to rise to great heights of accomplishments in his chosen field. He may even have a position of leadership although he is not gifted in that area. He is motivated more by the enjoyment of life, art, intellectual and cultural exchanges than by materialism, but his greatest and natural motivation is to become the focus of attention. In love matches, he is most attracted to the oldest sister of brothers and also oldest sister of sisters, women a few years older than he or persons with similar or identical sibling position as his mother. He may get along with a younger sister if she is considerable younger than he is. Marriage to another only child creates difficulties in that the two are unable to live up to each other's unconscious expectations for attention. He is not particularly motivated to be a father and may have some feelings of jealousy for the child, but in the end may pamper or overprotect his child. Male friends are less important to him than father figures.

Oldest Sister of Sisters

The oldest sister of sisters is a caretaker and order giver. She likes to be in charge, and derives her leadership position from another person in authority, often an older man or a man in a high position, like her father. She can remain unquestionably devoted to an older man of authority for long periods of her life. Material wealth and goods are less important to her than responsibility and power. She may seem intimidating to men who want to court her. It is hard for her to give in. A most amiable partner is the youngest brother of sisters, but she may criticize him for being soft or sloppy. A youngest brother of brothers will also be compatible. An oldest brother of sisters seems too conceited to her, because of his experience with other women, and she will find it hard to be emotionally intimate with an oldest brother of brothers. An only child could be her partner if he is flexible. She is not interested in men who held the same sibling position her father held. Children are more important to her than her husband, but the arrival of children may relieve any tensions existing in the marriage. Her need for authority and nurturing now has a more natural outlet. She may become overprotective and smothering to some extent. She loves the dependence of children. She may suffer from the empty-nest syndrome when they leave. At the same time, she may find it easier to forego marriage and family life altogether than other women do. Women friends are more important to her than men friends. She will experience a need to continue her contacts with women through the years, and her favorite friends will usually be younger sisters of sisters. Other compatible friendship relationships for her include only children, especially if they are a few years younger than she is or are daughters of mothers who are youngest sisters. She also understands other oldest sisters of sisters although these may not be close friendships.

The Youngest Sister of Sisters

The youngest sister of sisters is bubbly and impulsive, loving change and excitement. She is attractive and may find herself in competition with other women. She can be moody and capricious. She balks if someone tries to manipulate her. She will work hard for recognition and praise, loving to excel. She seeks guidance from other people, but not overtly. She is on a lifelong search for respect and can be quite sensitive about this. She tends to be suggestible but has the courage to take great risks. While she is interested in material things, she may be inconsistent in her efforts to amass things. She is ambivalent regarding men. While it is easy for her to attract a man, she may become competitive, especially if the man shows any tendency to take charge. Her best partner is an older brother of sisters. She may find it harder to get along with an older brother of brothers, although she may attract him more easily. An only child would be a poor match unless the man were considerably older than she or if his father were himself an oldest brother. The youngest sister of sisters may need family or hired help in her mothering. If her husband is helpful with the children, she will find mothering much easier. Her best woman friend will be an older sister of sisters or a middle sister who had a younger sister herself. She is also compatible with oldest and youngest sisters of brothers.

The Oldest Sister of Brothers

The oldest sister of brothers is independent and strong. She enjoys taking care of men and does not ask for much in return, except that the men around her be satisfied. The men in her life are her main concern. At work she often feels superior but does not show it. She can create an atmosphere that is appreciated at work. She can give advice to even the boss because she does not compete with men and actually may facilitate their relationships. She is less interested in women. She is optimistic and seems to need the companionship of men. Material possessions do not motivate her as much as possessing men, but she can administer properties and wealth well. She may be the sponsoring benefactor of gifted men. Her best marital partner would be the youngest brother of sisters, a younger brother of brothers, or a middle brother who has at least one older sister. An only child would work if his own father was himself a younger brother. An oldest brother of brothers may lead to a power struggle. She loves caring for children and may tend to favor sons over daughters. She may express occasional frustration with her husband's seeming passivity in the family. Friendships with women are unimportant to her, but the most compatible tends to be with the youngest sister of sisters.

The Youngest Sister of Brothers

The youngest sister of brothers is the most attractive of all the sibling positions to men. She is all that a man would conventionally wish from a woman; feminine, friendly, sympathetic, sensitive, and tactful. She is a good pal but may be a bit spoiled or extravagant. She is not ambitious for her own sake but may become so for the sake of an ambitious partner. She is not interested in work but can become motivated by the man she loves. Property and wealth do not interest her, but she is usually well taken care of by brothers or husband. The man in her life is her real wealth. She is attractive and charming to men and they instinctively seek her company. Her best marriage choice is ordinarily an oldest brother of sisters. A youngest brother of brothers or an only child would be the least favorable matches, especially if his father had been an only child or a youngest brother. She makes a loving mother but may be seen by her children as being too dependent or seductive. She is more interested in her husband than in her children. She fosters the role of gentleman and protector in her sons. Daughters learn well from her how to be feminine, impress men, subordinate oneself, or get what one wants from men. Women friends are not important to her. They may envy her for her good fortune with men and her long-lasting relationships with them, which come naturally to her.

The Female Only Child

As with the male only child, the female only child tends to structure her life around older people, people in authority, and superiors. Her strongest motivation is to obtain their approval and hopefully their preferential treatment. If she gets these things, she can be a good companion. Female only children tend to believe that their parents owe them help and support long into their adult years. Without a patron to champion her cause, her career may falter. Even with a patron, she may not do as well in a career as her male counterpart. Material wealth is not as motivating to her as the attention of a patron. She may be seen as spoiled or egocentric in her dealings with men. Her mother may assist her in matchmaking and may come as part of the package in her marriage. The female only child can be a good wife and is not inclined to become unfaithful. Her best partner would be the oldest brother of sisters. An oldest brother of brothers may provide the fatherly guidance she expects. A youngest or middle brother of sisters may offer her understanding of women and it will help if he is somewhat older than she. Unfavorable partners would be a youngest brother of brothers or a male only child, unless special circumstances prevailed or the spouses worked out a functional living arrangement rather than an intimate interaction. A greater-than-average age distance between the two would help, as would early identification of the husband with a father who had been an oldest sibling. A female only child prefers to be a child rather than to have children. If her mother or a mother substitute is available to help, her mothering will be facilitated. The female only child enjoys women friends, especially if they assume a motherly role toward her. She will enjoy the relationships more if they are older than she or if they are oldest sisters of sisters. She does better with individual contacts with her women friends than in groups.

Special Sibling Positions

In addition to the ten classical positions described by Dr. Toman, there are two other positions that, because of their complexity or infrequency, deserve special mention.

The Middle Child

Middle siblings may hold more than one role, since they relate differently to their younger and older siblings. Quite often one of these roles will be the strongest or will have been held for a longer period of time. This will continue to be the predominant role. In general, the siblings immediately adjacent to the middle child in age will be more important. In large families, siblings tend to form into subgroups. In such a case, a middle sibling may sometimes take on the characteristics of an oldest or a youngest.

Twins

As a rule twins live with each other from birth on and have experiences different from those of other siblings. As a result of family influences, one may function as the older—the senior in charge—and the other the junior— the impulsive and dependent one. They frequently meet the world as a pair, and they find it hard to imagine life without the other. When twins have other siblings, both of them take on the characteristic and behavior that an individual would in their sibling position. When the twins are, say, the oldest boys and have two younger sisters and a younger brother, they learn to take the roles of oldest brothers of brothers and sisters. When the twins are girls and have come after an older sister, both of them are likely to assume the features of younger sisters of sisters. Thus, they should be viewed as siblings in their relationships with each other, and they are likely to adopt the social behavior and interaction preferences that correspond to their overall sibling position.

The description of twins applies to triplets and quadruplets (which are rare enough to make common trends less easy to study), but their relationships to each other are more complex and variegated. They remain more detached from other siblings than do twins, and there is more environmental focus on them, which changes the family life significantly.

APPENDIX V

How Sibling Positions Combine in Relationships

How do the different sibling positions interact when they are combined in relationships? Dr. Toman's "duplication theorem" says: "other things being equal, new social relationships tend to be more enduring and successful the more they resemble the earlier and earliest (intrafamilial) social relationships of the person involved."[1] In his studies of thousand of relationships, Dr. Toman found that some combinations of sibling positions seemed to have an easier time making their relationships work, whereas other combinations were noncomplimentary and, therefore, required more work when combined in relationships.

Positions without Rank or Sex Conflict

There are two position mixes that are totally complementary. They are:

Oldest Brother of Sisters and Youngest Sister of Brothers
This is usually a good relationship. These two people understand each other, rarely quarrel, and supplement each other in tasks. If they marry and have children, they will be attentive and thoughtful parents. The father will set the tone in the household, but he is friendly and tolerant, while the mother is soft and submissive.

Youngest Brother of Sisters and Oldest Sister of Brothers
This, too, is a good relationship with good mutual understanding between the two; the woman is the one who sets the tone for the relationship. The man likes the woman's advice and needs her encouragement. If these two marry and have a family, they will usually agree on issues concerning the children. She makes most of the decisions but keeps him informed. He usually consents.

Partial Sex Conflict

Four relationship patterns have a partial sex conflict. They are:

Oldest Brother of Sisters and Youngest Sister of Sisters

This is a relatively good relationship. Though the woman may have some trouble getting used to living with a man, he can usually teach her. She may oppose him or compete with him, but struggles are short-lived. He sets the tone in the family and she obeys him—with occasional balkiness. She will need to continue contacts with her women friends and sisters.

Youngest Brother of Sisters and Oldest Sister of Sisters

This relationship is relatively good. These two are prone to get along with each other, although consorting with a male peer requires adjustment on her part. She is slightly more authoritarian than he would like, but his sense of humor will win the day. She sets the tone in the family, perhaps a bit too seriously. If they marry and have children, the children may ally with their father and feel he is one of them. The woman is interested in justice and order in her family. She must have the opportunity to keep up her feminine contacts and stay busy with some responsibilities outside the family.

Oldest Brother of Brothers and Youngest Sister of Brothers

A relatively favorable relationship. He may be too tough or self-righteous with her and inadvertently treats her as a younger brother. She usually knows how to tone him down however, and so, in time, be becomes more open to her concerns. This is partly taught to him by her brothers. He enjoys pleasing her, and if they marry and have a family he may learn to satisfy his leadership needs more at work and with their children. He will need to maintain contacts with male friends on regular terms throughout his life.

Youngest Brother of Brothers and Oldest Sister of Brothers

Again, a relatively good relationship. The man is a follower as long as he is not patronized. He is able to accept a woman's leadership and guardianship more willingly than a man's. She may tend to mother him. He wants most of all to be understood. She treats him like one of their children, if they marry and have children. His sense of humor sometimes makes for surprises. He will continue to desire contact with male friends throughout their relationship.

Rank or Sex Conflict Relationships

There are four relationships that have either rank or sex conflicts. They are:

Oldest Brother of Sisters and Oldest Sister of Brothers

This relationship is moderately favorable. These people have learned to live with peers of the opposite sex when growing up, but both of them are oldest siblings, so they will tend to get into power struggles with each other. Each wants the other to give in, and each finds it difficult to do that. Dividing their tasks may help things.

Youngest Brother of Sisters and Youngest Sister of Brothers

This relationship is moderately good. Each person is experienced with peers of the opposite sex, but each is looking for leadership and responsibility from the other. Neither seems quite capable of providing this. Each was dependent on a sibling of the other sex while growing up. Each requires understanding but does not feel understood.

Oldest Brother of Brothers and Youngest Sister of Sisters

A moderately favorable relationship in which both people complement each other by the age rank of their sibling positions. Since the man is the oldest and the woman the youngest, the problem of neither of them having a sibling of the opposite sex is somewhat ameliorated. He tends to take the lead in this relationship, but their situation remains tense for a rather long time, although it can be exciting in the beginning. She wants his advice and leadership role and yet finds herself resenting it from time to time. If they marry and have children, she accepts a female relative's help readily. It is important for both people to maintain contact with their same-sex friends.

Youngest Brother of Brothers and Oldest Sister of Sisters

A moderately good relationship, although neither he nor she has experienced a relationship with an opposite sex sibling while growing up. He submits to her leadership, which may be unnecessarily strict or brusque. He will occasionally compete with her until he feels listened to by her. If they marry and have children, they do not agree on how to advise them. Both partners will need to retain contact with their same-sex friends and acquaintances.

Rank and Partial Sex Conflict Relationships

There are four relationship positions with rank and partial sex conflicts. They are:

Oldest Brother of Sisters and Oldest Sister of Sisters

This is a more difficult relationship. The partners will tend to be engaged in a power struggle. The woman has not been accustomed to life with a peer of the opposite sex, and she is not very prone to learn this from her husband. He tends to be more sympathetic and tolerant, and she more rigid and strict. She will enjoy not giving up her job or career completely if they marry and have children, but it will work best if they don't work together.

Youngest Brother of Sisters and Youngest Sister of Sisters

Again, a difficult relationship because only the male has learned in his original family how to deal with a peer of the opposite sex. However, his expectations for nurturing and care rather than opposition, leadership rather than competition, may be frustrated. The woman is not sure whether to compete or submit. She tends to be critical of her husband's inadequacies. She may keep searching for an older brother to serve as an extra friend.

Oldest Brother of Brothers and Oldest Sister of Brothers

A difficult relationship because both are order-givers and responsible and both find it difficult to give in. Only the woman has been accustomed to life with peers of the opposite sex as she grew up. She could give guidance in this, but her husband is unlikely to listen. If they marry and have children, he will be more strict and she will be more lenient. They will each need juniors and dependents to care for. Their conflicts with each other will be reduced if they pursue their own interests independently.

Youngest Brother of Brothers and Youngest Sister of Brothers

A difficult relationship because only the woman knows from her experience while growing up how to handle a peer of the opposite sex. Both partners, being youngest, are searching for guidance and parental attention, but neither knows how to give it. He may be looking for a woman, as an additional friend, who is an older sister. She may need support from one of her brothers.

Rank and Sex Conflict Relationships

There are two relationship patterns with both rank and sex conflict. They are:

Oldest Brother of Brothers and Oldest Sister of Sisters

An unfavorable relationship because their own sibling experiences have not prepared either partner for life with a peer of the opposite sex. Also, there is a rank conflict for both; each will expect the other to submit, but neither is qualified for that role. Their conflict may be described as a battle of the sexes. Separate careers may help the situation. They will each need to retain their same-sex friends throughout the relationship. Temporary leaves from each other and separate rooms may help also. If they marry and have children, their relationship may seem to improve although they will be exacting parents and tend to recruit the same-sex children into alliances.

Youngest Brother of Brothers and Youngest Sister of Sisters

Again, unfavorable because of sibling experiences that put them in a relationship where both, being accustomed to being taken care of and guided as they were growing up, will tend to expect more leadership from the other than is naturally possible. Each also has had no experience living with a peer of the opposite sex. The partnership lacks leadership and direction for decision-making. If they marry, having children will not make life much easier for them. They may find some direction in their own extended families. Separate professions, interests, and pursuits of talents independently of each other may help. They will also need to maintain same-sex friendships on a fairly regular basis.

Only Children

Only children in relationships will probably do better if they marry someone who has had sibling exposure while growing up and try to learn about how to get along in peer relationships. The only child relating in a marriage will be especially helped by a partner who has had peers of the opposite sex. If both people in the relationship are only children, they will both be looking for a parental friend in a relationship but will rarely find it. At least they can identify with one another in the longing to have parental approval. Because of this identification, they may develop a smoother relationship. If two only children marry and have a child, they may tend to concentrate more intense hopes in the child than do other parents.

Endnote

1.   Toman, Walter, *Family Constellation*. Springer Publishing Company, New York, 1976, p. 80.

INDEX

About the Author

Dr. Gilbert is a psychiatrist whose primary interest is in Bowen family systems theory and its applications and extensions. She is a Distinguished Retired faculty member of the Bowen Center for the Study of the Family, (formerly Georgetown University Family Center) after serving in many capacities there. She served on the clinical faculties of the medical schools of Georgetown University, University of Kansas, and University of Missouri at Kansas City.

For many years, Dr. Gilbert has directed leadership training for clergy and other leaders of organizations in the Extraordinary Leadership Seminar. Her last three books were texts for that seminar.

She speaks and teaches master classes for leaders and therapists nationally. She also speaks by Skype and Zoom to national and international groups.

Dr. Gilbert lives in Florida where writing, music, travel, friends and community activities compete for her time.

She is a woman with a mission: "to make this wonderful new way of seeing the human from a broader perspective—Bowen family systems theory—as accessible to as many people as possible."

Notes

Notes

Notes

Notes

Notes

Notes

Notes

Notes

Made in the USA
Coppell, TX
02 August 2021